D6 Family Ministry Journal

Published by Randall House Academic
www.randallhouse.com

Editors

Ron Hunter Jr., Ph.D.
Executive Editor

Michelle Orr
General Editor

Charles Cook
Managing Editor

Editorial Board

John Trent, Ph.D.
Gary D. Chapman Chair of Marriage and Family Ministry and Therapy at Moody Theological Seminary

Timothy Paul Jones, Ph.D.
Associate VP and Professor of Family Ministry and Applied Apologetics at Southern Baptist Theological Seminary

Ron Davis
Chair of Bible Department
at Southeastern Free Will Baptist College

Mike Butler
Professor of Ministry

Ken Coley, Ed.D.
Professor of Christian Education and Director of Ed.D. Studies at Southeastern Theological Seminary

Steve Vandegriff, Ed.D.
Professor of Youth Ministries at Liberty University

Chris Talbot
Professor and Program Coordinator for Youth & Family Ministry at Welch College

Leneita Fix
Speaker, Author, and Founder of Urban Life Resources

Heidi Hensley
Speaker, Author, and Children's Ministry Guru

Adam Clagg, Ed.D.
Pastor, Author, Former Adjunct Faculty in Bible, Ministry, and Critical Thinking

Purpose Statement

The purpose of *D6 Family Ministry Journal* is to support the thinking and practices of parenting in Christian homes, in family ministry in the local church, and in parachurch settings that reflect God's intent for generational discipleship as presented in Deuteronomy 6 and other biblical texts. This purpose is achieved by the publication of articles and essays that do the following:

- Reflect on the scriptural foundations of God's use of paternal and maternal influences in the lives of children and grandchildren while also acknowledging various contemporary family situations
- Explore the integration and application of the relationship between the church and home
- Support the teaching of generational approaches to Christian education at colleges and seminaries for the equipping of ministry leaders and parents
- Champion methodologies that prepare children and young adults in the development of a Christian lifestyle and Christian leadership skills

The journal is primarily intended for two audiences: an academic community of professors and students in institutions of higher learning who are committed to the development of a new generation of Christian ministers and community leaders. Second, those professionals who are already serving in local church and parachurch settings. In order to facilitate discussion and learning among both groups, each publication will:

- Provide publishing opportunities primarily for:
    ◦ academic peer reviewed work
    ◦ practitioner reflection
- Offer a platform for research into family ministry
- Review new books connected to generational discipleship and classic texts and family ministry related fields

Manuscripts for publication should be directed to the attention of the managing editor at the following address: 114 Bush Road, Nashville, TN, 37217. Email inquiries should be sent to academic@d6family.com.

© 2017 by Randall House Academic
Printed in the United States of America
ISBN 9780892659951

Volume 2   June 2017   D6 Family Ministry Journal

Contents

Editorial

Introduction   1

Articles

Community and Completion in the Relational Reading   3
of the Imago Dei: A Family Ministry Application
Shawn Crawley

Pastoral Demands and Resilience Characteristics   17
Edward E. Moody Jr. and *Chadwick Royal*

Early Southern Baptist Views on the Baptism of Children   29
Robert Matz

Family, Love, and Duty in Narnia   51
John F. McCard

Singles: Our Forgotten Families   65
Jackson Watts

Practitioner Insights

Counseling Christian Teens Struggling With Same-Sex Attraction   83
by Ken Coley

A Practical Strategy for Partnering With the Family by Phil Bell   93

The Role of Games in Discipleship by Jon Forrest   101

Ministering to Widows and Widowers With Children in the Home   105
by David Lytle

Book Reviews

The Millennials by Thom S. Rainer and Jess W. Ranier   111
   Nashville, TN: B&H Books, 2011.

Youth Ministry in the 21st Century: Five Views by Chap Clark, Editor   115
   Grand Rapids, MI: Baker Academic, 2015.

Editorial

The *D6 Family Ministry Journal* strives for one overarching goal. That goal is to bring scholarly research and the best practices in Church and Home ministry together. The scholarly research assists practitioners in recognizing what practices work best under what conditions. The practitioners' insights help other ministry participants to see how responding to certain opportunities and challenges will affect the work they do. Under this overarching rubric, bringing scholarly research and best practices together, the editors and Journal board anticipate readers determining that the D6 Journal's 2nd edition is a wonderful asset.

The 1st Journal edition sought to include original scholarly research. Fortunately, that trend continues in this edition with a piece by Eddie Moody on pastoral demands and resilience. Pastoral ministry is unquestionably demanding work, and it is important for ministers, congregants, and the pastor's immediate family to understand the ways in which the unique work of the pastor effects individuals and families, physically and emotionally. In Moody's work readers will find a helpful blend of research and practicality.

While Moody's article focuses on pastoral demands and the effects of such demands on pastors, the piece by Jackson Watts highlights the prospects and difficulties facing singles participating in local churches. The piece also looks at complicating factors awaiting those churches that embrace the challenge of singles ministry. Jackson's piece is especially useful in helping identify singles that do not fit what is often thought of when the phrase singles ministry is used. With Jackson's section, another future trend of the Journal is hopefully developing, the ongoing importance of recognizing overlooked groups and individuals in the Church and Home discussion.

Whereas Jackson and Moody address concrete challenges facing the church and home, the article by Shawn Crowley begins with an important theological and biblical concept, the "Imago Dei" and seeks to show how understanding the biblical and theological centrality of God's Image can and should shape family ministry. In his approach to this topic, Crowley engages with some important academic theologians from the last 100 years. As a Journal committed to the centrality of God's Word in Holy

Scripture, it is not surprising that part of the discussion of faithful Home and Church ministry revolves around the biblical texts. However, Crowley infuses a resource into the discussion, the insights of scholarly church theologians on how theological concepts can inform practical ministry.

If Crowley's piece enters into an oft neglected space of Church and Home dialogue, the section by Dr. McCard breaks entirely new ground for the D6 Journal. Among families, stories frequently play a foundational role in shaping how home life is conceived and transmitted. For 21st century American Evangelicals, few stories for children have made the impact of the Narnia novels of C. S. Lewis. McCard does readers a favor in his article by showing the strengths and limitations of Lewis' view of the family as presented in the Narnia tales. Given the impact of Lewis on the American imagination, this area of research deserves more future attention.

As readers will see, whether the article is research dominated, theoretical in nature, or one of our reflection pieces, it is a joy to see the Journal's 2nd edition published. It is the prayer of the publisher, editors, and board that the *D6 Family Ministry Journal* will continue to assist those engaged in Church and Home ministry. May God bless the reading and the ministry of readers wherever that reading and ministry may take place.

Charles Cook

Community and Completion in the Relational Reading of the Imago Dei: A Family Ministry Application

Shawn Crawley

Andreas Kostenberger asserts that despite the proliferation of workshops, ministries, para-church organizations, media, and resources, there is a conspicuous absence of a solid, cohesive biblical theology regarding issues of marriage and family (Kostenberger & Jones, 2010, p. 19). While elements of this are increasingly apparent in writing on family ministry, most of these works still seem to focus more on the pragmatic aspects of doing family ministry. Deeper doctrinal considerations of anthropology, soteriology, and eschatology, specifically with respect to families and family ministry, largely seem to lie on a still distant horizon (Anthony & Anthony, 2011 and Stinson & Jones, 2011 are two examples to the contrary). Such a deficit leaves the Church under-equipped to most meaningfully and accurately address the ultimate significance of God's design for humanity in the realm of human relationships.

One example of this deficit, encompassing a diverse range of interpretation, regards the image of God in created humanity. What, exactly, does it mean that both man and woman are created in God's image? What are the traditional interpretations of this, and what is the significance of each in both doctrine and application; how does this impact our understanding of relationships? More generally, to the end for which Kostenberger and others advocate, how can we wrestle with these ideas fruitfully for the purpose of better shaping our ministries? The answer to this last question shapes preaching, counseling, premarital preparation, youth ministry, and other family ministries in the Church.

As family ministry continues to be studied, defined, and practiced, the necessity to think clearly about undergirding doctrine also becomes increasingly important. At Creation, for example, God instituted the family and gave it foundational meaning. The image of God was found in both man and woman, observable to one another in the lives they lived out in front of one another in Paradise. And in procreation, they brought other images into the world as well (Lawson, 2011, p. 70). Thus, ministry to families in all cases is also ministry to those that bear God's image. A clear understanding of the linkage between a strong theology of humanity and a strong theology of family could best inform ministry practice in this regard. How can this anthropological consideration shape what we do? In light of that question, it is the purpose of this essay to consider one particular family ministry approach in light of an anthropological issue, in order to illustrate how the larger theological principle finds expression in the practical exercise of family ministry. It is proposed that the principles of completion and community as found in the relational view of the *imago Dei* are specifically expressed in the church-as-family approach to family ministry.

Understanding the Relational *Imago Dei*

Traditionally, there have been three main schools of interpretation of the concept of the *imago Dei*, each one emphasizing different aspects of the Scriptural teaching (Grudem, 1994, pp. 445–449). One of these views, the Relational Understanding, highlights the relational capacity held by humanity, both amongst itself and between humanity and God. Most prominently articulated by Karl Barth, this view considers the potential symmetry between the triune God—God in relationship to Himself—and the relationship between male and female in the created order. The image of God is best captured in the interrelationship of the Trinity, and is best mirrored in the relationship between male and female, according to Barth (Hammett, 2007, p. 373). It is this key principle of relationality that is also a central aspect of the church-as-family approach to family ministry examined later in this article.

On the sixth day of Creation, God says something different than He has on the previous days. The first clue that something different is about to happen is when the Creator, rather than instructing Creation to take this or that form, says, "Let us make..." (Gen. 1:26). A subtle but significant statement that what is to come is different from all that has already happened has now appeared in the text (Sailhamer, 1990, p. 37). Humanity is created and then given the charge to exercise dominion over the rest of Creation. The particular language emphasized here is vital to defining and understanding the issue. In Genesis 1:26-28, the biblical account speaks of humanity being created in plurality (He created *them*), by a God who speaks in plurality (*our* likeness) (Dennis, 2007). Interpretation requires grappling with at least three questions here. First, what exactly does the image of God mean or represent? Secondly, what is the significance of God speaking in a collective or plural sense? Thirdly, what might either of these have to do with how man and woman are to fulfill the mandate to exercise their given dominion?

Particular terminology for "image" rarely appears in Scripture, making an easy understanding elusive (Wenham, 1987, p. 29). Because Hebrew terms connoting both physical likeness and qualitative likeness appear in these verses, it is not eminently clear what this means for created humanity. The Hebrew term *tselem* connotes a physical manifestation or representation of God on the earth, such as a statue or marker. The term *demut* carries a more essential understanding, whereby humanity bears the image of God in a representative sense. Man carries God's authority and dominion over His Creation as a vice-regent figure (Hoekema, 1994, p. 13). Anthony Hoekema and others suggest that these terms are interchangeable, and in fact represent the notion of a more complete imaging of God. Others, as we will see below, suggest that the unique terminology does carry different meanings. The point here is not to resolve this particular question, only to bring to light this issue: how one understands the Hebrew language here will impact how one interprets the meaning of the *imago Dei*. If *tselem* (physical likeness) is correct, this would more easily suggest that humanity bears God's image in a functional sense. Man is to have more tangible, functional similarity to God, perhaps in the actual exercise of the dominion over Creation prescribed in Genesis 1:26-27. On the other hand, if *demuth* is more correct, this suggests that there is an essential (though not inherently divine) similarity between Creator and Created. There is something about the inherent qualities of humanity that somehow reflects God Himself (Hoekema, 1994, p. 13).

What, then, of the language of plurality used in Genesis 1:26-28? Is God plural? If so, in what sense? A reading of only the English might suggest that God is both male and female. How can God the Father be female? But an exegetical exploration of the question clearly leaves room to support a relational interpretation that is permitted via the original Hebrew terminology. Man (*adam*) is created in plurality (male and female—*zakar unqebah*) in a similar sense as the one God performed the creative act in an expression of His own plurality (*naseh adan bsalmenu*—let us make man in our image.) This was intended to show the relationality of male and female as parallel to the interrelatedness of God within Himself (Sailhamer, 1990, pp. 37–38).

Finally, there is the connection between the meaning of God's image and what its proper role in Creation is. The fact that both male and female are specifically included in verse 27 makes clear that both male and female bear the image of God. The way this is done also makes clear that what comes next is directly related to this understanding. The distinction of male and female also anticipates the unveiling of fertility as a creation blessing (Wenham, 1987, p. 33). There is clear connection between the image of God as seen in both male and female, and in the command to "Be fruitful and multiply and fill the earth and subdue it…" (1:28). The linkage has to do with the institution of the family in Creation. This motif is extended later in Genesis 5:3, when Seth is named as a descendant of Adam, being both his image and likeness. He is both biological descendant, and heir to the same creation blessing of procreation as was his father Adam; thus, the family perpetuates the *imago Dei* (Matthews, 1996, p. 170).

This relational view, then, addresses how humanity uniquely bears God's image in Creation, that both male and female bear this image, and that this is essential to the creation of the family.

Community and Completion in the Relational View

Community in the Relational View

Karl Barth, Dietrich Bonhoeffer, Emil Brunner, and other neo-orthodox theologians have articulated various understandings of this view. The most prominent exposition of this idea comes from Barth. Barth offers an elaborate explanation of the image of God in man in Vol. III, Part 2, of his *Church Dogmatics, The Doctrine of Creation*. True and real humanity, he asserts, is only rightly known in Jesus Christ, in whom it is possible to live in God's grace as His chosen covenant partner (Barth, 1986, pp. 221–222). Barth makes a two-pronged argument relevant to this point. First, he contends that since the image of God manifested in Jesus was basically His being-for-others, this means that the basic form of humanity is a being-with-others in particular relationships. More particularly, it means the specific determination of this being with others in the relationship of man and woman. The basic form of humanity is humanity in relation to itself; I to Thou, according to Barth (Barth, 1986, p. 285).

Inherent in God's expression of Himself in humanity is the difference between male and female. Secondly, and more narrowly, it is not the expression of the sexual differences between man and woman so much as it is the free giving of one's self to another that is key (Barr, 1982, p. 477). This relational correspondence between man and woman again mirrors a God who is in relationship with Himself. As the Father, Son, and Holy Spirit are always in relationship and fellowship to each other, humanity is in the same way created by God as fellow-humanity (Barth, 1986, p. 324). Thus, the *imago Dei* is not the uniqueness of gender, or the fruit of the relationship, as much as it is the relationality of one to another. This same thought can also be seen in the interdependent characterization of the body of Christ as expressed in passages such as 1 Corinthians. 12. This idea finds even more clear expression in the "mystery" that is Christ and the Church as expressed in Ephesians 5 (Macdonald, 2008, p. 305). To put it colloquially, the whole is greater than the sum of the parts. In light of this, it seems clear that this view points to *community* as the expression of the image of God in Man.

Dietrich Bonhoeffer frames the idea with the notion of freedom. Humankind images God in that it is free. Particularly, man is free to worship God the Creator (Bonhoeffer & de Gruchy, 2007, pp. 62–63). However, Bonhoeffer argues, this freedom only makes sense if it is understood to exist and to be expressed in relation to another. I am only free when I am free to give myself to another in relationship to them; freedom without an object is not freedom (Bonhoeffer & de Gruchy, 2007, p. 63). Bonhoeffer connects the concepts of man imaging God and doing so specifically by relating to another. This expression of love, empowered by the Holy Spirit and directed at God the Creator is mirrored by the love between man and woman, given freely in mutual interdependence (Bonhoeffer & de Gruchy, 2007, pp. 63–64). The *imago Dei* is realized in man, Bonhoeffer argues, when human relates to human, particularly here man to woman in marriage, as Created does to Creator.

Bonhoeffer adds force to the idea that it is not what the relationship accomplishes that is paramount, but the very relationship itself. That would be to say that the *imago Dei* is rightly understood as an expression of community. It is the essential need for another in order to rightly image God that Bonhoeffer proposes. That is not to say that relationships for their own sake are the proper understanding of the *imago Dei* in humanity. It would be to say that relationships between man and woman intentionally reflect God's relational existence within Himself and with humanity. Community understood in this way is inherently an expression of God in Man.

More contemporarily, Bruce Ware comments that while male and female are co-equal as image bearers, their individual roles within that understanding differ. There is a designed order of interrelatedness of male and female within the Creation narrative that now manifests itself in both home and household of faith (Ware, 2002, p. 92). Ware links complimentary gender roles in both family and community of faith to the issue of the *imago Dei*. This complementarity is not the focus of the thought here, but Ware's application in this way also affirms that the relationship between male and female is itself a particular expression of God's design. Thus, the degree to which human relationships do image the Creator is the degree to which we can understand the Trinity itself as informing our understanding of humanity as *imago Dei*. Ware seems to build upon Barth and Bonhoeffer in inviting consideration of how human relationships, with respect to roles and responsibilities, reflect the community of the Trinity itself. This question of living out anthropological reality in human relationships thus now stands squarely in the domain of family ministry.

Completion in the Relational View

Building on interpretations emphasizing the *locus classicus* in Genesis 1, Raymond Ortlund and others help a second principle to emerge. Where the principle of *community* draws out the conceptual issue, the principle of *completion* deals with the practical outworking of that community. The central question revolves around Genesis 2:18; when God pronounces that something is not good. How could it be that someone (Adam) in unimpeded fellowship with a perfect and holy God, in an uncorrupted setting, would have any kind of deficit? One answer seems to lie in the expression of the relationship inherent in the principle of community. In a response to a contemporary feminist assertion, Ortlund refutes the notion that both genders are required to fully image God. Citing Genesis 5:1 and 5:3, he makes clear that good exegesis does not allow for God's perfect Creation to be essentially inadequate (Ortlund, Jr., 2006, pp. 98–99). It is instead a question of expression. It was in executing his God-given service in Eden that man discovered his need for another (Ortlund, Jr., 2006, p. 100).

Understanding Genesis 2:15-25 as an elaboration of 1:26-27 opens the door to understand the concept of completion in the relational view. If community is a legitimate implication of the relational view of Genesis 1:26-27, then completion, rightly understood, follows from there. Kostenberger seats the act of creating woman in God's sovereign benevolence. Nothing in the text suggests Adam knew any sense of discontentedness in his singleness. Rather, God acted on his own knowledge of Adam's state, according to Kostenberger (Kostenberger & Jones, 2010, p. 25). Timothy and Kathy Keller also affirm God's graciousness to a finite creation. We need relationship with others by design, going clear back to paradise; being alone was indeed not good (Keller & Keller, 2011, p. 111). Werner Neuer appeals to complementarity, echoing Bonhoeffer and Barth, when he observes that in Genesis 2 it is clear that woman comes from and is for man to be his suitable helper (Neuer, 1991, p. 63). She comes into existence to both complete and help him (Neuer, 1991, p. 73). Such commentary makes this principle very clear: that which bears the image of God, has not only capacity but need for relationship. So much so, that woman is identified as being created for man for that purpose.

There is another, admittedly secondary, aspect to consider regarding the notion of completion that adds a very practical element to this concept. Christopher Ash reminds us that there is still the work of attending to Creation to be accomplished (Ash, 2003, p. 121). Despite man's essential completeness in an uncorrupted world, Adam can still best fulfill his created purpose with Eve's help (Ash, 2003, p. 120). Despite the unmistakable relational context, it is impossible to completely escape the functional side of Eve's role as a suitable helper. While this functional aspect is not the primary focus of this language, its presence adds force to the overall idea of completion.

On the whole, three implications seem permissible and helpful regarding the issue of completion. First, the key to rightly understanding this principle appears to have to do with completion as an expression of community, not an inherent characteristic. It is active, not passive, in terms of imaging God. Adam was not essentially flawed and incapable of imaging God in either the *tselem* or *demut* sense on his own. It is in the expression of relationship, much as Bonhoeffer argued, that the potential becomes actualized; the imaging of God is evidenced in the relationality of man. Adam needed another in order to be able to visibly represent the relationality of God with Himself. It could be said that Eve completed the imaging of God, in this sense.

Secondly, these ideas have numerous specific implications for the greater meaning of our relationships. Given this, what does man learn about his Creator in living with woman? In thinking about marriage, what does a wife learn about the patience or the forgiveness or the graciousness of God when she experiences patience, forgiveness, or graciousness from her husband? What does a husband better understand about his God when he sees longsuffering commitment and generous affection that his wife extends to him? Perhaps to a lesser degree (perhaps not), what does a child learn from a parent in the same way? What does a single adult learn from his or her close community and family of faith in the same manner? Conversely, in any of these relationships, what understanding of God is impaired by the absence of another? Are there things about God that can only be grasped by engagement in relationship? To some degree, while affirming the primacy of marriage in this interpretation, this principle generalizes to include children, singles, and others in loving community. It seems that understood as expression, the imaging of God to each other in relationships, marriage included, is a very real aspect of the principle of completion.

Finally, for all the conceptual discussion about completion, it is important to remember the practical aspect of woman's creation as suitable helper for man; the work given to them in Creation. Man and woman hold essential and complementary roles in God's created order for the purpose of accomplishing God's purpose in the world. Humanity has the highest privilege in that we are given dominion and prominence above all other created beings in this physical world, in order to bring glory to God through our lives here. This is the very clear, important teaching of Genesis 1:26 and 28; while our time here is brief, we are created for a purpose. In accomplishing that purpose, two are better than one. (Ecclesiastes 4:9).

With the concepts of community and completion within this view now examined, how this can inform the practice of family ministry is now considered.

The Church as Family

Chap Clark identifies three general approaches to family ministry (Clark, 1997, p. 14). Among them is the "church-as-family" perspective, a broad-based idea of family ministry that intentionally cultivates the idea of the local church as a family unto itself. The goal of all ministries in such a congregation is to integrate members into a family and community of faith within that given local body (Clark, 1997, p. 18). Central to this approach are ministries that give soul care (therapeutically focused Bible studies, counseling services, support groups, etc.), for the purpose of making people whole individually, through their identity in Christ, before linking them in healthy relationships within nuclear families and within the broader church body (Clark, 1997, p. 18). The end of family ministry in this approach is to do all that a church does so its members experience ongoing, vibrant family-like community together (Garland, 2012, p. 121). This approach, and others like it, reflects the idea of completion as a necessary precursor to or aspect of community. In this way, the relevance of the relational view of the *imago Dei* quickly intersects with the practice of family ministry.

As people find healing in their lives and relationships, the desire exists to participate in a larger group, to be a part of a faith family. Charles Sell suggests that this is no less than the nature of the church. Any ministry done in the lives of people must always be recognized to occur in a context of interrelatedness that shapes the congregation as a whole. For Sell, the necessary context for real family ministry is a church that understands itself to be a family (Sell, 1995, p. 157). While such churches certainly invest in the meeting of needs both inside and outside of the congregation, the defining characteristic of congregations following this framework is Community. Diana Garland defines family ministry generally as that which forms families within the congregation and then moves them towards Christlikeness (Garland, 2012, p. 120). The work of healing and strengthening of families points naturally to the formation of community with others like them. This echoes of the connection between completion and community explored above.

It is important to note, however, that community is not the end unto itself in this approach. Closer examination of this approach suggests that the function or role, as well as the meaning of that function or role of family units, are the definitive elements here. Dennis Guernsey suggests that the Church be understood as a system of interrelated and interdependent family units; a family of families (Guernsey, 1985, p. 100). Because God designed the family as the fundamental unit in creation, it is necessary for the Church to take into consideration how to address intra-familial relationships. This is a matter of utmost priority for Guernsey, who suggests that failure to engage people with the gospel in their relationships represents a failure to bring the full weight of that gospel to bear on their condition (Guernsey, 1985, p. 66). Even beyond the redemptive aims of healing and salvation, this understanding of the church and family in balance seeks to address the relational context in which all people exist irrespective of actual relational status. Guernsey and others argue for the primacy of relationships as a vehicle within which to minister people toward wholeness (Guernsey, 1985, p. 178). The work of family ministry in congregations ministering with this goal in mind consists of, amongst other objectives, helping to develop an authentic sense of belonging amongst individuals and family units within that local body (Guernsey, 1985, pp. 106–109). This again links completion and community.

A more contemporary impetus for the church-as-family approach comes from the Emergent movement. Eddie Gibbs and Ryan Bolger define nine elements of the Emerging church, among them a renewed emphasis on living as intentional community. Such communities emphasize relationships over tasks and meetings, and most closely resemble a family in their efforts to embody the family of God as defined and demonstrated by Jesus Himself (Gibbs & Bolger, 2005, p. 97). This emphasis on community in the Emerging church is largely a response to the perception of the contemporary Western church as materialistic, or more specifically consumeristic and individualistic. Such cultural values have impacted the Church, it is thought, at a detriment to the solidarity of strong families such as were found in the early Church. Joseph Hellerman suggests that a return to the idea of the Church as a kind of surrogate family is needed to reverse trends in the contemporary church toward consumerism and transitive affiliation. Without such an emphasis on authentic community of this kind, we should expect to remain thirsty for real renewal as the people of God (Hellerman, 2009, pp. 8–9). Such a community will espouse certain values such as: priority of the group over the individual, the primacy of blood family, and the unique strength and place of the sibling bond even over the marital one in terms of the larger community (Hellerman, 2009, p. 50). These priorities will be expressed in the sharing of possessions and in the close details of everyday life, as well as forbearing interpersonal difficulties for the sake of growing up together and having a family that ultimately extends beyond nuclear family relationships (Hellerman, 2009, p. 162).

This approach incorporates both the meeting of needs and the formation of families as intentional aims, but the meaning behind those aims clearly runs far deeper than just giving individuals or family units of any kind a soft place to land spiritually. Guernsey, Hellerman, and others like them illustrate the depth of the relationship between church and family, and the formative element inherent within that connection. This church-as-family approach helps move people toward healing and wholeness in Christ and intentionally places them within a larger supportive context.

This brief survey suggests how churches using this approach to family ministry, by doing things such as teaching relationship skills, offering small groups based on life stage, forming family care groups and the like, can be quite effective in helping people find a way to integrate into Body life via family connections. The importance of integration into the Body with the goal of forming gospel community is apparent here. The distinct nature of such community is intentionally formative more than merely social. This speaks to both community and completion when considered in light of the relational interpretation of the *imago Dei*. Part of the role of those others in my world is to be used by God to cultivate my deeper identity in Him. My relationality, addressed here through ministries intended to grow and heal my relationships, forms the crucible for my Christoformity; my relationships in the sense of my most immediate community are where I most directly image God. God's image in man understood as an increasing Christlikeness is the starting point for family ministry according to Garland, for example, but occurring quite definitively in the context of community.

While full exploration is beyond the scope of this particular conversation, this survey alludes to the role of things like therapeutic, support group, and skill building kinds of ministries to families. There is a wealth of these available to the Church today. The intention of this survey was to consider how a relational understanding of the *imago Dei* can inform the practice of these kinds of family ministry theologically, not just pragmatically. In defining the relational view, original Creation, and the deep, rich, meaningful significance of man imaging God in his relationships with both his Creator and with humanity is considered. In applying it, how this can be brought into practical consideration in the Church and family together is examined. The relational view allows for this consideration through the principles of community and completion. The church-as-family approach to family ministry seeks to cultivate both.

References

Anthony, M. J. *A theology for family ministries.* Nashville, TN: B&H Academic, 2011.

Ash, C. (2003). *Marriage: Sex in the service of God.* Vancouver, B.C.: Regent College Publishing.

Barr, W. R. (1982). Life: Created in the image of God. *Mid-Stream, 21*(4), 473–484.

Barth, K. (1986). *Church dogmatics: The doctrine of creation.* (G. W. Bromiley & T. F. Torrnace, Eds.) (Vol. III, Part 2). Edingurgh: T & T Clark.

Bonhoeffer, D., & de Gruchy, J. W. (2007). *Creaton and fall: A theological expostion of Genesis 1-3.* (D. S. Bax, Trans.). Minneapolis, MN: Augsburg Fortress Press.

Clark, C. (1997). *Youth worker's handbook to family ministry.* Grand Rapids, MI: Zondervan Publishing House.

Dennis, L. T. (2007). *ESV Study Bible.* Wheaton, IL: Crossway Bibles.

Garland, D. R. (2012). *Family ministry: A comprehensive guide* (Second). Downers Grove, IL: InterVarsity Press.

Gibbs, E., & Bolger, R. K. (2005). *Emerging churches: Creating Christian community in postmodern cultures.* Grand Rapids, MI: Baker Academic.

Grudem, W. (1994). *Systematic theology: An introduction to biblical soctrine.* Grand Rapids, MI: InterVarsity Press.

Guernsey, D. B. (1985). *A new design for family ministry* (Second). Elgin, IL: David C. Cook Publishing Co.

Hammett, J. S. (2007). Human Nature. In D. L. Akin (Ed.), *A Theology for the Church* (pp. 340–408). Nashville, TN: B&H Publishing Group.

Hellerman, J. H. (2009). *When the church was a family.* Nashville, TN: B&H Academic.

Hoekema, A. (1994). *Created in God's image.* Grand Rapids, MI: William B. Erdman's Publishing Co.

Keller, T., & Keller, K. (2011). *The meaning of marriage: Facing the complexities of commitment with the wisdom of God.* New York, NY: Dutton.

Kostenberger, A., & Jones, D. W. (2010). *God, marriage, and family: Rebuilding the biblical foundation* (Second). Wheaton, IL: Crossway Books.

Lawson, M. S. (2011). Old Testament Teachings on the Family. In *A Theology for Family Ministries* (pp. 66–87). Nashville, TN: B&H Academic.

Macdonald, N. (2008). The Imago Dei and election: Reading Geneses 1:26-28 and Old Testament scholarship with Karl Barth. *International Journal of Systematic Theology*, *10*(3), 303–327. http://doi.org/10.1111/j.1468.2400.2007.00283.x

Matthews, K. A. (1996). *Genesis 1-11:26* (Vol. 1). Nashville, TN: Broadman & Holman Publishers.

Neuer, W. (1991). *Man and woman in Christian perspective*. Wheaton, IL: Crossway Books.

Ortlund, Jr., R. C. (2006). Male-Female equality and male headship: Genesis 1-3. In J. Piper & W. Grudem (Eds.), *Recovering Biblical Manhood and Womanhood: A Response to Evangelical Feminism* (Second, pp. 95–112). Wheaton, IL: Crossway Books.

Sailhamer, J. H. (1990). Genesis. In *The Expositor's Bible Commentary* (Vol. 2, pp. 1–284). Grand Rapids, MI: Zondervan Publishing House.

Sell, C. (1995). *Family ministry* (Second). Grand Rapids, MI: Zondervan Publishing House.

Stinson, R., & Jones, T. P. (Eds.). (2011). *Trained in the fear of God: Family ministry in theological, historical, and practical perspecive*. Grand Rapids, MI: Kregel Publications.

Ware, B. (2002). Male and female complementarity and the image of God. In *Biblical Foundations for Manhood and Womanhood* (Vols. 1–4, pp. 71–92). Wheaton, IL: Crossway Books.

Wenham, G. J. (1987). *Genesis 1-15* (Vol. 1). Dallas, TX: Word Books.

Author Biography

Shawn Crawley is a graduate student at The Southern Baptist Theological Seminary.

Pastoral Demands and Resilience Characteristics

Edward E. Moody, Jr. and Chadwick Royal
North Carolina Central University

Author Note: Edward E. Moody, Jr. is Chair of the Department of Allied Professions, and Professor of Counselor Education at North Carolina Central University in Durham, North Carolina and Pastor of Tippett's Chapel Free Will Baptist Church in Clayton, North Carolina. Chadwick Royal is an Associate Professor of Counselor Education at North Carolina Central University in Durham, North Carolina. Correspondence regarding this article may be sent to emoody@nccu.edu or Dr. Edward E. Moody, Jr., North Carolina Central University, Department of Allied Professions, School of Education, 700 Cecil Street, Durham, North Carolina, 27707.

Abstract: The demands that pastors face have been well documented. This study examined the pastoral demands and resilience characteristics of a sample of Free Will Baptist ministers. Descriptive statistics were used to analyze the data. Results indicated that the top barriers experienced were disappointment (43%) and conflict (34%). Overall, the sample felt fulfilled in the ministry ($M=7.85$). They felt most comfortable sharing their difficulties with their spouse (64%), followed by another pastor (45%), and a friend (24%). In general, they believed their work in the ministry had a positive impact upon their families ($M=7.8$).

Keywords: Pastors, Ministry, Resilience, D6

An Examination of the Pastoral Demands and Resilience Characteristics of a Free Will Baptist Minister Sample

Serving as a pastor is a very demanding calling. Many years ago the Fuller Institute of Church Growth presented results of a survey from pastors that was very alarming. More than 80 percent of pastors surveyed felt that the ministry had negatively impacted their family, 50 percent reported dropping out of full time ministry within five years, 70 percent said they did not have a close friend, and 37 percent acknowledged being involved in an inappropriate sexual behavior in the church (Headington, 1997). Such information leads one to wonder if pastoral ministry is toxic, and if so, what can be done to mitigate the risk?

Certainly the multifaceted nature of the pastoral role places enormous strain upon the minister and their family. Pastors often begin their work early in the morning and return home after late evening meetings. Many are called in the evening to deal with a crisis and most know the feeling of being called home from a vacation to conduct a funeral. Clergy are well acquainted with illness, death, and trauma of their congregants, which some have described as an unseen cost of ministry (Hendron, Irving, & Taylor, 2012). Additionally, pastors often experience unrealistic expectations and lack an adequate extra-familial support system. Stressors often include financial strain, lack of privacy, always being on call, and a diminished quality of life (Meek, McMinn, Brower, Burnett, McRay, Ramey, Swanson, & Villa, 2003).

It sounds like some clergy engaged in the trenches of ministry are so consumed by their work that they do not do a good job of taking care of themselves (Seaman, 1998). Some may feel trapped by their calling. Perkins (2003) noted that while few ministers commit physical suicide, many commit ministerial suicide. Ministerial suicide was described as a way to quit ministry without being a quitter. Sometimes this is done by losing one's temper in a public setting or engaging in sexual immorality.

In particular, pastors seem to be especially vulnerable to sexual temptation. Balswick and Thoburn (1991) found that the ministerial role was especially vulnerable to sexual temptation because of the emotional emptiness felt by single, divorced, or unhappily married women in which the minister frequently interacted. The problem is further complicated because of the expectation for ministers to be sympathetic and understanding. These caretaking demands can lead to sexual encounters. The dynamic is further complicated for the minister who is seeking emotional and ego fulfillment. Pastors appear to have a high need of support on a more personal and intimate level, increasing their vulnerability (Seaman, 1998).

Developing Resilience

The role of pastor is critical to the growth and health of the church. In light of the importance of pastors, and the demands and inherent risk of the position, it is important that we help pastors develop resilience. What are the keys to developing pastors who can survive and thrive in the ministry?

One key to increasing resilience among pastors is to have strong relationships. Henry, Chertok, Keys, and Jegerski (1991) examined the stress experienced by Protestant ministers. They found that good relationships between the pastor and his family helped mitigate emotional triangles and stress symptoms. Pastors often view their spouse as their primary support system. In one study, 62 percent of respondents indicated that family relationships (spouse and/or children) were key in maintaining their emotional and spiritual health. Some of the pastors reported spiritual activities (praying, Bible reading together) were an integral part of the marriage (Meek et. al., 2003). Balswick and Thoburn (1991) found that a good marital and sexual relationship between the minister and his wife were critical to resisting sexual temptation.

Friendships

Another key to resilience is friendship. In one study, peer relationships, where ministers were held accountable, greatly reduced their susceptibility to the demands of the pastorate (Balswick & Thoburn, 1991). In another study, friendship was spontaneously endorsed by 42 percent of pastors as a key to resilience, which was followed by an opportunity to be mentored and held accountable (35 percent). When asked about the most important thing a denomination could do, 45 percent of the pastors mentioned the need to be mentored and known by others. It also appeared that many pastors needed to hear they were valued and needed to be listened to, which helped reduce burnout (Meek et. al., 2003).

Perhaps the most stressful situation for a pastor is to be terminated from a church. Carver (2001) examined ministers who had been forcibly terminated from the church and found they experienced less anxiety initially and were more resilient when they had higher levels of peer support (Carver, 2001). A study of Hungarian Baptist pastors indicated that those with accountability partners were less susceptible to burnout. The author inferred that a comprehensive systematic approach was needed to help pastors deal with stress.

Learning Focus

McKenna, Boyd, and Yost (2007) found that resilient pastors were able to learn from their experiences (both positive and negative) by adopting a learning focus. As they attempted to navigate their role they tended to rely on their calling and character while learning ways to establish and manage relationships. Another study indicated that key life lessons for pastors were learned during significant transition (27%), and that most pastors felt they were often working on the edge of their comfort zone (McKenna & Yost, 2007).

Balance

Meek et al. (2003) quoted a pastor as an example of resilience who said, "It's not the things in ministry that kill you, it's the things you don't get done—every night you leave you know that there's another twelve people you should call, another three books you should read, another eight people that you need to visit in the hospital" (p. 342). To address this urgency resilient pastors were intentional about creating balance and boundaries in their lives. This includes separating oneself at times from their role as pastor. One pastor noted, "I avoid becoming financially or emotionally dependent on the church" (p. 342). It appears that a key is to be intentional about crafting time away from pastoral duties and not becoming a workaholic (Meek et. al., 2003).

Spiritual Disciplines

The spiritual disciplines are a key component to resilience as the role of prayer and spiritual discipline has been found to be a key to avoiding temptation in pastors (Balswick & Thoburn, 1991). In one study, sixty-six percent of pastors indicated that retreat/solitude, reading the Bible, journaling, fasting, and prayer were key to dealing with stress (Meek et. al., 2003). In another study, the spiritual disciplines, hobbies, and exercise were found to be key for pastors to cope with the demand of ministry, along with their relationship with their spouse and family. On the other hand, relationships outside the immediate family were not nearly as often identified (McMinn, Lish, Trice, Root, Gilbert, & Yap, 2005).

Pastors must be intentional about protecting themselves, their family, and their marriages, and taking time for themselves and to engage in the spiritual disciplines. In this study, we will examine the barriers experienced and the resilient characteristics of a sample of Free Will Baptist ministers.

Method

Participants

The participants in this study were senior pastors of the National Association of Free Will Baptists that were approached in two southern states at their state association or ministerial retreat and asked to complete the survey. A total of 42 completed the survey. All of the participants were male, they had pastored a mean of 3.4 churches for a mean of 19.46 years, they had spent a mean of 6.3 years as an associate pastor. See Table 1 for sample characteristics.

Table 1

Sample Characteristics

Characteristic	df	M	SD
Number of Churches pastored	41	3.4	2.6
Number of years in the pastorate	38	19.5	13.5
Number of years as associate pastor	29	6.3	6.4

Instrument

The *Survey of Pastoral Life* was created for this study after being piloted with pastors in another country. In addition to demographic information, the survey questioned pastors about their emotional state, their confidence sharing difficulties with others, and challenges and difficulties experienced in the ministry. Descriptive statistics were used to analyze the responses.

Procedure

The study was approved by the Internal Review Board at North Carolina Central University and permission was obtained from the promotional directors from the two states where the pastors were surveyed. Pastors were approached at denominational meetings and asked to complete the surveys.

Results

Descriptive statistics were used to examine the emotional state, barriers experienced, comfort sharing difficulties as well as impact upon the family of the sample.

Emotional State

Pastors were asked to rate their emotional state on a scale of 1 (very unstable) to 10 (very stable). Overall, the pastoral sample viewed themselves as being emotionally stable. They reported their current emotional state as stable ($M=8$), their emotional state over the past year was also reported as stable ($M=8$), as well as stable over the course of their ministry ($M=7.92$). Participants were asked to rate their feeling of fulfillment in the ministry on a scale of 1 (very unfulfilled) to 10 (very fulfilled). They reported feeling fulfilled in the ministry ($M=7.85$). Participants provided reasons for their response and some of the most listed responses are found in Table 2.

Table 2

Fulfillment or nonfulfillment in Ministry

Sample reasons for feeling unfulfilled in the ministry
Not seeing anticipated results.
I should be doing more.
Lack of church growth.

Sample reasons for feeling fulfilled in ministry
I am where God wants me to be.

The good far outweighs the bad.

Progress that has been made and the peace that comes from my Heavenly Father.

Mixed reasons for feeling fulfilled or unfulfilled in ministry
Change isn't coming as quickly as I'd like, but I see God working.
I love to pastor, but I always feel like there is more we should do.

Struggles and Barriers Experienced

The main struggles the pastors reported experiencing included disappointment (43%), conflict (34%), depression (26%), money problems (24%), and sexual temptation (22%). See Table 3.

Table 3

The biggest barriers faced in the ministry

Barrier	Percentage that endorsed
Disappointment	43
Conflict	34
Time Constraints	29
Adequate Preparation	26
Depression	26
Money	24
Sexual temptation	22

Pastors were asked to rate whether sexual temptation was a challenge to them on a scale of 1 (strong disagree) to 10 (strongly agree). They reported slightly in the direction of agree ($M=5.9$). When asked whether they had a strategy to deal with sexual temptation on a scale of 1 (strong disagree) to 10 (strongly agree), they reported in the direction of agree ($M=8.1$). Regarding temptation, the respondents reported yielding to internet pornography (30.9%), pornographic magazines (18.9%), and inappropriate videos/DVDs (18.4%).

Comfort Sharing

When asked about their comfort sharing their difficulties with other pastors, the pastors were less enthusiastic $(M=6.5)$. However, when asked specifically who they were currently sharing their difficulties with 45.2 percent reported sharing their difficulties with another pastor. The most frequent mentioned person that they could talk to was their spouse (64%) followed by a friend (21%). See Table 3.

Table 3

They share their difficulties with . . .

Person	Percentage
Spouse	64
Another pastor	45
A friend	24
Other	
Deacon	05
No one	05
The Lord	05
Parents	02

When asked to provide reasons why they did not feel confident talking to other pastors, sample was nearly unanimous in reporting a fear of confidentiality being violated. The most frequent responses are found in Table 4.

Table 4

Sample reasons given for hesitancy to share difficulties with pastors

Confidentiality concerns
Because of embarrassment and lack of close friendship with another pastor
I'm afraid of what they would think or say to others
Fear they may lose respect for me
They do not really listen

Don't trust many, you would know next Sunday's sermon
In my experience it has been pastors you cannot trust
Many have a judgmental attitude
Lack of close relationship with another pastor
No need to burden them with other difficulties

Impact Upon Family

Pastors were asked to rate whether the ministry had resulted in a positive impact upon their family on a scale of 1 (strongly disagree) to 10 (strongly agree). They reported in the direction of the ministry having a positive impact upon their family ($M=7.8$). In a sentence completion section, they acknowledged they treat their family well but occasionally falter (50%), look nice at church but not at home (38%), look happy and nice at church but not at home (7.1%), and what you see at church is what you see at home (4.76 %). When asked about how supportive their spouse was in the ministry, pastors rated their wives as very supportive ($M=9.03$). Indeed, this sample appeared to take time with their family each week. Average time spent weekly with family was indicated as follows: 1 hour (2.3%), 5 hours (11.9%), 7 hours (2.3%), 10 hours (21.4%), 15 hours (9.5%), and more than 15 hours (30.9%). When asked whether they spent at least one day each week with their family, pastors responded in the strongly agree direction ($M=7.2$).

Spiritual Disciplines

Pastors reported on the amount of time they spent weekly praying as follows 1-5 hours (21.3%), 6-10 hours (61.7%), and over 10 hours (15.2%). Pastors reported on the amount of time they spent doing weekly personal devotions as follows 1-5 hours (16.6%), 6-10 hours (47.4%), and over 10 hours (33.24%).

Discussion

In many ways, the findings from this study were consistent with previous research on pastors. Some of the main barriers in the ministry were disappointment and conflict. This sample of pastors relied primarily upon their wives to confide in regarding the difficulties they experienced. Less than half felt comfortable discussing their difficulties with other pastors, and based on the response section of the survey, many of the participants had been negatively impacted from confiding in other pastors in the past. Consistent with other research on pastors was the small number (25%) who indicated they had a friend with whom they could discuss their difficulties.

This is a mature sample ($M=19.5$ years) with many years in the pastorate. It would be interesting to see how younger pastors might respond. It was refreshing to see that though they did indicate their service in the ministry had been challenging, they did not feel unfulfilled or that the ministry had negatively impacted their family in contrast to the Fuller Institute of Church Growth sample. Though they had struggled with sexual sin, they had not succumbed as severely and the majority reported having a plan for dealing with sexual temptation. The key elements of resiliency seemed to be present. They confided with their spouse and overall families seemed to have fared well in the ministry. They also seemed to be doing well in the area of the spiritual disciplines. We did not assess whether they had a learning focus, which has been found to be a key component of resilience. There are areas where more work is needed.

Based on these results it appears the Free Will Baptist denomination would benefit from more work in the area of mentoring. The biggest concern expressed by this sample involved not being able to talk to other ministers. Many reasons were given. Most were concerned about a lack of confidentiality, but there were other concerns like other pastors not having time for them or judging them because of their need. Based on previous research, pastors have expressed a desire for (and appear to have greatly benefited from) mentoring. As we see it, this could take place in two directions. The first would be from the direction of our colleges. It would be helpful (if it has not been done already) to set up a way to mentor new graduates the first 5 years out of graduation. We realize many pastoral graduates do not proceed directly to the pastorate (and many who end up in the pastorate were not pastoral majors), but beginning to have a process where a graduate is checked in with on a monthly basis could form the foundation of a strong mentoring relationship whenever the graduate reaches the pastoral field.

A second prong to address this issue is through the state and local association, especially since many who find their way in the pastorate either did not attend college or are far removed from that training. Mentoring should be a requirement (or at least strongly suggested) when candidates appear before ordination committees, especially since it has been found to be so effective.

It should be noted that this is a small and mature sample as one attempts to make generalizations. However, since they are more mature one might conclude that they are a bit healthier than those with 1-5 years of pastoral experience. Future research should be conducted on that population to examine their specific needs. It is important that we do as much as we can to develop resilient pastors to effectively perform the critical calling they have received from the Lord.

References

Balswick, J., & Thoburn, J. (1991). How ministers deal with sexual temptation. *Pastoral Psychology, 39*(5), 277-286.

Carver, H. G. (2001). An investigation into the effects of force-termination on Southern Baptist ministers' stress responses and coping resources. *Dissertation Abstracts International: Section B: The Sciences and Engineering, 61*(10-B), 5609.

Giorgiov, A. D. (2002). The effect of accountability on pastoral stress and burnout among select Hungarian Baptist pastors. *Dissertation Abstracts International Section A: Humanities and Social Sciences, 63*, 992.

Headington, G. L. (1997). A guide to recovery for fallen pastors: The journey back from sexual misconduct. Unpublished doctoral dissertation, Fuller Theological Seminary, Pasadena.

Hendron, J. A., Irving, P., & Taylor B. (2012). The unseen cost: A discussion of secondary traumatization experience of clergy. *Pastoral Psychology, 61*(2), 221-231.

Henry, D., Chertok, F., Keys, C., & Jegerski, J. (1991). Organizational and family systems factors in stress among ministers. *American Journal of Community Psychology, 19*(6), 931-952.

Perkins, E. (2003). Ministerial suicide. *International Journal of Reality Therapy, 22*(2), 38-43.

McKenna, R. B., Boyd, T. N., & Yost, P. R. (2007). Learning agility in clergy: Understanding the personal strategies and situational factors that enable pastors to learn from experience. *Journal of Psychology & Theology, 35*(3), 190-201.

McKenna, R. B., & Yost, P. R. (2007). Leadership development and clergy: Understanding the events and lessons that shape pastoral leaders. *Journal of Psychology & Theology, 35*(3), 179-189.

McMinn, M. R., Lish, R. A., Trice, P. D., Root, A. M., Gilbert, N., & Yap, A. (2005). Care for pastors: Learning from clergy and their spouses. *Pastoral Psychology, 53*(6), 563-581.

Meek, K. R., McMinn, M. R., Brower, C. M., Burnett, T. D., McRay, B. W., Ramey, M. L., Swanson, D. W. & Villa, D. D. (2003). Maintaining personal resiliency: Lessons learned from evangelical Protestant Clergy. *Journal of Psychology & Theology, 31*(4), 339-347.

Seaman, R. L. (1998). A comprehensive assessment of clergy self-care practices among active parish clergy members of Monmouth presbytery. *Dissertation Abstracts International Section A: Humanities and Social Sciences, 59*, 0205.

Author Biography

Edward E. Moody, Jr. is Chair of the Department of Allied Professions, and Professor of Counselor Education at North Carolina Central University in Durham, North Carolina and Pastor of Tippett's Chapel Free Will Baptist Church in Clayton, North Carolina.

Chadwick Royal is an Associate Professor of Counselor Education at North Carolina Central University in Durham, North Carolina.

Early Southern Baptist Views on the Baptism of Children[1]

Robert Matz

A narrative has been posited among Southern Baptists regarding the history of child baptismal practices. Specifically, it has been asserted that the practice of baptizing children is novel among Southern Baptists with earlier generations of Southern Baptists historically preferring to delay the baptism of children.[2] The argument for the novelty of child baptism has been made through appeals to studies showing declining average ages of baptism,[3] through appeals to increasing rates of preschool baptisms,[4] and through appeals to the baptismal ages of specific historic individuals.[5] Yet none of these methodologies provides a complete picture of the child baptismal practices among earlier generations of Southern Baptists. Specifically, the statistics cited from the late nineteenth and early twentieth century to show a declining average age of baptism are flawed as they utilized studies that did not look at the practices of Baptists.[6] The claim regarding increasing rates of preschool baptisms is overstated as the number of preschool baptisms has always been insignificant compared to the number of total baptisms[7] and because the number of preschool baptisms is actually declining.[8] Utilizing the age of baptism of a group of select notable Baptist individuals is problematic because such a list is not representative of Southern Baptists as a whole and because an alternative list has been offered.[9]

Therefore, this article offers a new line of examination into the views of early Southern Baptists regarding child baptismal practices. Specifically, it offers an examination of the written views of early Southern Baptists regarding the possibility of child conversion and the appropriateness of child baptism.[10] In so doing, it will establish that despite claims of novelty, many early Southern Baptists were actually open to the baptism of children.

The Views of Early Baptists in the South Regarding Children and Baptism

The child baptismal practices of Baptists in the South, prior to the formation of the Southern Baptist Convention, are difficult to determine. Direct references to the age at which children were baptized during this era are scarce.[11] As Hugh Wamble notes, the emphasis of the Baptistic literature of this era is "on repentance from sin and faith towards God, both expressed voluntarily and publicly, as indispensable qualifications [for baptism]. Literature is silent about age."[12] Compounding this issue is the fact that the terms "infant" and "child" are often used interchangeably in older Southern Baptists literature. Further, the term "adolescent" is foreign to many older texts.[13] Thus, the authors' views of early baptism regarding children are normally found in the implications of their writings and not in their direct statements.

The Charleston Baptist Association's *A Summary of Church Discipline* was a relatively influential document among churches in the South in the eighteenth century. It is silent to both the age of baptism and the role of children in the faith community. The document does imply that baptism should be contemporaneous with faith profession stating "baptism is by immersion *upon* a profession of their faith, agreeable to the ancient practice of John the Baptist and the apostles of our Lord."[14] The document also affirms the need for "an entire change of nature" and to restrict church membership so the "unconverted, unbelievers, and graceless persons" are not able to usurp control of the church. From such restrictions, Wamble implies that children may have been excluded, yet still concedes that Baptists have been more interested in defining the qualifications for admission into a church than in setting an age at which such could occur.[15]

I. T. Hinton who pastored in churches in both the North and the South stands as the rare example of one who directly writes about child conversion and baptism during this era. In the context of paedobaptist arguments arising from household baptismal practices in the New Testament, Hinton is open to the conversion and baptism of children. He states "prove to me that a child believes in God in the Gospel sense of that phrase, and I ask no questions about its age."[16] Still, Hinton expresses hesitancies, asking a few sentences later if it would "not be better for all children to wait till they give good evidence that they love the Saviour?"[17] Yet, Hinton does not indicate how long this delay should be or what constitutes good evidence.

One of the primary areas children are explicitly addressed in the writings of early American Baptists is within the educational literature of that era. The histories of various Baptist conventions provide documentation of this. These histories note that the religious education of children was closely tied to the religious education of adults. For example, according to one historian of early South Carolina Baptists, the "instruction of children in the principles of religion does not seem to have received general attention as distinct from adults."[18] In similar fashion early Tennessee Baptists' "children were taught religion, morals and work."[19] From these accounts it is clear that children were religiously schooled from an early age and were instructed in the same materials as adults. Only with the rise of the Sunday School movement would an emphasis on separate curricula for children develop.[20] For purposes of this study, it is significant that early Baptists believed that children should be exposed to the same religious instruction as adults. Still, determining a specific age at which early Baptists of the South understood children as valid candidates for baptism cannot be determined.

The Views of Nineteenth Century Southern Baptists Regarding Children and Baptism

In 1845 in Augusta, Georgia, the Southern Baptist Convention was formed as a result of northern Baptists[21] prohibiting southern Baptist slave owners from engaging in mission work.[22] During its early years, the convention formed its own seminary, mission boards, and publication society. The pastors, theologians, and denominational employees of this new convention quickly set to work producing literature, much of which was geared toward the doctrine of baptism and its appropriate candidates.

While still uncommon, direct statements regarding child baptismal practices began to appear.

One of the most significant direct treatments regarding the baptism of young children during this era comes from Richard Fuller. Fuller was a well-known Baptist pastor in Baltimore and author of the influential treatise on baptism, *Baptism and the Terms of Communion*, which was originally published by the Southern Baptist Publication Society. In it, Fuller explicitly argues that young children can be baptized and included in church membership. Commenting on when infants should be baptized, Fuller states "when old enough, it would still be the duty of the child to believe and be baptized in obedience to the commission"[23] Fuller clarifies what he means by "when old enough" in the context of his debate with Dr. Kurtz, a paedobaptist. Kurtz has apparently argued from Acts 16:33 for paedobaptism, saying, "young children themselves of four or five years of age rejoice" in their knowledge of the gospel and salvation. To this assertion Fuller responds that "babes [that] are old enough to know spiritual joy, and to utter praises to God! Such infants as these I shall be happy to baptize everyday of my life."[24] Thus, Fuller asserts that he would baptize a four or five year old who utters praises to God. For Fuller then children can be converted and if and when this occurs, they should be baptized.

Still, Fuller is cautious. He warns against manipulating children into conversion saying "worlds could not tempt me to act in [securing God's blessing for] my child, unless I had God's clear warrant for it."[25] He also further clarifies his view of infants stating that "to talk about preaching the gospel to infants is to use the language of insanity."[26] Thus, for Fuller, infants cannot grasp the gospel. Despite his hesitancy as to the salvation of infants in a generic sense, Fuller distinguishes between four- and five-year-old "infants" who can have a saving faith and should be baptized, and those infants who cannot hear the gospel and thus cannot be saved.

John A. Broadus, who was the second president of the Southern Baptist Theological Seminary, also argued for the conversion and church membership of young children. He states: "We hold that the Christian Church ought to consist only of persons making a credible profession of conversion, of faith in Christ. These *may include children, even comparatively young children,* for God be thanked that these do often give credible evidence of faith in Christ! But in the very nature of the case, they cannot include infants."[27]

Baptist pastor, theologian, and President of Mercer University, J. L. Dagg offers direct comments dealing with an age of initiation. Expounding upon Ephesians 6:1, Dagg argues for the full membership of children within the church stating,

> The probability is, that the children whom Paul addressed were members of the church. The command, "Obey your parents in the Lord," [Eph. 6:1] is so expressed, as apparently to imply that the obligation was to be felt and acknowledged by them, because of their relation to the Lord. The children to whom Paul addressed this command must have possessed intelligence to apprehend its meaning, and piety to feel the force of the motive presented in these words, "For this is well pleasing unto the Lord." ... Intelligent piety has, in all ages, been found in children who have not yet reached maturity; and *such children have a Scriptural right to church-membership*.
>
> The argument that the children were so young as to need the care and discipline of their parents to bring them up in the nurture and admonition of the Lord, does not prove that they were destitute of personal piety.[28]

Therefore, for Dagg, young children who exhibit "personal piety" are not only to be baptized, but also are to be part of a regenerate church.

Basil Manly Jr., who helped found Southern Seminary and the first iteration of the Southern Baptist Sunday School Board, also argued for the conversion of young children. Manly argued for the addition of Sunday School to the curricula of Southern Baptist churches in part because "the early conversion of the children is rendered more probable" by their presence.[29] While he concedes that some are skeptical about the ability of children to be converted and that there are risks in children not being thoroughly converted, he responds stating that "there is nothing more attractive, nothing more desirable, nothing for which I am more willing more ardently to labor, and which I will more eagerly expect until it is accomplished, than the conversion of children."[30] He also sees a significant risk in children not being converted early in life in the time lost for service to Christ. "Let us not esteem lightly so many years of youth saved from the service of Satan and spent in the service of God."[31]

James Petigru Boyce, the founding president of the Southern Baptist Theological Seminary, addresses children both briefly in the body of and again more specifically in the appendix to his *Abstracts of Theology*. Within the body of the *Abstract*, Boyce assumes the cognitive abilities of children to grasp the gospel. First, Boyce notes that children have always had the ability to learn about God and as a result come to belief in him. He states "belief in God has been handed down from parent to child throughout all past generations."[32] Second, Boyce substantiates this claim noting how children come to this belief at a young age through asking questions and the parent's convictions. He states "this is the natural manner in which every child among us learns about God. [The child's] own questionings, or its parent's convictions of the importance of this knowledge cause [the child] to be imparted at an early period, and by direct teaching of the fact alone without proof."[33] Thus, for Boyce, children can grasp Christian belief.

As a result, it is unsurprising that Boyce desires to help parents and churches in the conversion and discipleship of their children. Specifically, he wants to make sure that children ages 10-12 are theologically grounded. Therefore, he provides a new catechism as an appendix to the *Abstract*. Therein, he notes that "Keach's Catechism...is scarcely used at all... [because] it is too difficult for children. In the present work...my aim has been to bring the truth taught within the comprehension of children of ten to twelve years old and upwards."[34] In offering this catechism to 10 to 12 year olds Boyce implies that such persons are valid candidates for conversion and church membership. This takes on special significance given the argument cited in the introduction that the typical age of baptism during this era was between 15 and 20. While as was shown above, such claims are suspect, if one were to grant them, then Boyce, in offering a catechism to 10 to 12 year olds, is assuming that conversion and baptism should happen at a younger age then was commonly accepted. Still, Boyce's direct views on the timing of baptism as it relates to the conversion are less clear as he offers no section on such.

While Fuller, Broadus, Dagg, Manly Jr., Strong, and, to a lesser extent, Boyce all directly address the theological status of children, other influential Baptists leaders' views from the era on either children or the immediacy of baptism are less clear. Still, their views imply a positive view as to the possibility of child conversion and baptism. For example, influential Baptist pastor and newspaper editor J. R. Graves does not deal directly with a child's relation to the church, but instead indirectly addresses the issue of child baptism in his theology of baptism. He states that baptism "is a visible expression or declaration that faith exists, it simply expresses or professes…faith."[35] He continues, stating that "our baptism authenticates our faith, [and] declares us as believers."[36] Ultimately, "salvation is essential to baptism,"[37] and if a saved person chooses not to be baptized they are ashamed of Christ and are acting in disobedience.[38]

Elsewhere Graves addresses the baptism of children while addressing paedobaptism. He states, "to place baptism upon…an unconscious infant is to pervert the ordinance and to teach a falsehood, which if the…child so baptized should believe, would insure the loss of the soul."[39] Graves elaborates on this idea explaining that children baptized as infants will develop a false sense of security at a young age. Dependence upon such theology damns the child early in life.[40] Given that children can gain a false assurance and be damned from such at an early age, according to Graves, it follows that for Graves (although he does not directly state this) that accountability occurs at an early age. Taking his assumption of early accountability together with his instance that a refusal by a believer to be baptized is a sign of disobedience, it follows logically that children can become Christians at an early age (since they can be damned at an early age) and if and when they do so, they should be baptized.

Another influential theologian whose views on the baptism of children can only be ascertained through incidental references is B. H. Carroll, a Texas pastor and founder of Southwestern Baptist Theological Seminary. Carroll states clearly his church's baptismal requirements. He "requires… converts applying for baptism evidence…that he is a child of God by regeneration, is a consistent believer, pardoned, saved. Without this evidence we will not baptize him."[41] Carroll, like all Baptists, insists that baptism occurs after salvation. Carroll also tells of a Methodist minister who "baptized a bright and promising young boy." Carroll, while not condoning Methodist baptism, nevertheless seems to indicate that such a boy is an appropriate candidate for baptism.[42]

Edmund Hiscox also shows a similar openness to the baptism of children. In addressing the paedobaptist argument that household baptisms included children, Hiscox states:

> If in those households any children were baptized, they were old enough to receive the gospel and to believe on Christ, and were thus suitable subjects for the ordinance, and for church fellowship. For it is said, "They believed, and gladly received the word." There are thousands of Baptist churches into whose fellowship whole households have been baptized parents and children, and perhaps others connected with them. But all were old enough to believe and to make profession of their faith. So evidently it was in these households.[43]

While Hiscox does not specify the age of these children,[44] his claim that "There are thousands of Baptist churches into whose fellowship whole households have been baptized parents and children" indicates that many late nineteenth century Baptists understood household baptism to include children.

In contrast to the theologians and scholars mentioned above, Southern Baptist pastor and graduate of the Southern Baptist Seminary, Henry R. McClendon, explicitly stands against the baptism of children. He looks to the church father Tertullian. McClendon states that "the earliest known allusion to the baptism of 'children' is found in Tertullian." Tertullian, he says, does not use the word for infants but rather for small children—"the baptism [of which] he opposes."[45] As a result, McClendon rejects the baptism of young children.

Ultimately, a pattern emerges during these early years of Southern Baptist life. Southern Baptists' most prominent academics and leaders at a minimum widely permitted and perhaps even endorsed the baptism of young children. Fuller, Broadus, Boyce, Basil Manly Jr. Dagg, and Hiscox all either assumer or argue for the baptism of children at an age younger than others have asserted was common during this era. Further, Graves and Carroll imply that young children can be converted. Additionally, Baptists theologians such as Graves and Fuller directly tie baptism to obedience, with it possibly even functioning as the profession one makes in response to salvation. To claim, as John Hammett does, "that Baptists prior to the twentieth century were slow to see childhood decisions as faith commitments warranting baptism" ignores the writings of numerous prominent nineteenth century Southern Baptists.[46]

Early Twentieth Century Southern Baptists Views Regarding Children and Baptism

At the turn of the century, Southern Baptists were a people in transition. From 1900-1925 the convention grew rapidly,[47] adding boards, a more permanent funding mechanism and in 1925, its first confession of faith.[48] In this setting, most Baptist leaders addressing the role of children in the church echoed the leaders of the previous generation. Yet E. Y. Mullins offered a new line of reasoning regarding the role of children in Southern Baptist churches.

It would be hard to understate E. Y. Mullins' influence on Baptist life in the first half of the twentieth century. Mullins served as president of the Southern Baptist Theological Seminary and was the primary author of the SBC's first confession of faith, The Baptist Faith and Message (1925). His *Axioms of Religion: A New Interpretation of the Christian Faith* stands as perhaps the most significant Baptist theological work of his generation. Mullins's primary contribution (for better and worse) to Southern Baptist theology was his emphasis on Christian experience as providing an appropriate foundation for Christian belief through the doctrine of soul competency.[49]

Within the *Axioms of Religion*, Mullins includes a chapter on Christian nurture. After noting the contradictions inherent in Calvinistic understandings of paedobaptism[50] he turns his attention to the Christian child. His entire discussion is oriented around a dialogue with Horace Bushnell's understanding of Christian nurture.[51] Specifically, Mullins rejects Bushnell's position that an infant's unity with his family requires that the infant be united to the church just as the parent is united to the church. Affirming credobaptism, he argues that "baptism belongs to the stage of intelligence and personality, to the stage of tuitional influences, and not to the stage of unconscious impressions."[52] As a result, a child must become cognitively aware of his environment and of his sin prior to conversion and baptism.

Therefore, Mullins argues, contra Bushnell that a child must become conscious of his own sin prior to salvation and baptism in order to come to salvation. While children may avoid grosser forms of sin, it is important to note that intellectual assent to the Gospel is insufficient to bring about the Christian life. As a result, Mullins rejects the practice of recitation of the catechism (contra Boyce?) as evidence for salvation.[53] Instead, children should be baptized when "there is recognized the presence in the child of a permanent Christian motive and struggle."[54] While not stating it directly, Mullins implies that this occurs at the age of 12. He notes that

> Jesus as a boy of twelve, upon the occasion of his first visit to the temple,...[felt] for the first time the great and wondrous significance of the Jewish system...upon [his] sensitive soul... Doubtless there was an awakening in his soul, a calling forth thus of the powers that were in him, and a quickening into a new sense of his mission and destiny...Even so should it be with childhood ever—expose the soul of the child to the truth, surround it with every incentive to holy living, permit it to respond to grace in the home circle.[55]

Mullins thus equates Jesus' experience in the temple with the awakening of a child's soul. Although not stating it directly, in so doing Mullins implies that 12 stands as an age of accountability.

From this point, Mullins closes his discussion of children by noting the need to bring the elements of Christian character into the child's conscious experience as early as possible. This occurs through the child's experience of religion, art, and science.[56] Given the surrounding references to science and to Jesus' temple experience, Mullins is not contradicting himself. Rather, he is arguing that children should be nurtured in knowledge of Christianity and as soon as they are conscious of the experience of religion (which apparently occurs at 12 at the earliest), they are valid candidates for conversion and baptism. Thus, Mullins restriction of child baptism to those twelve and older based on the cognitive sciences marks a notable shift in the thought of Baptist leaders during the first part of the twentieth century.

Unlike Mullins, most other Baptist's leaders of this era continue to express or imply an openness towards the conversion and baptism of young children. For example, J. M. Frost, head of the Baptist Sunday School Board (the Southern Baptist publishing arm), produced two treatises on baptism. Within them, Frost does not directly address the issue of the age of baptism. He does, however, address both childhood salvation and the timing of baptism. Specifically, he dedicates a whole chapter to the subject matter of the relation between baptism and conversion: "The New Birth and then Baptism."[57] Frost stresses that baptism's "prime purpose… is obedience to Christ, an acknowledgement of his reign in the new life."[58] Further, baptism "cannot be overemphasized so long as we count it the act of obedience of a saved person."[59] Frost does give an order to when baptism should fall in a new believer's life, pointing out that baptism should be preceded by regeneration, repentance, faith, and the remission of sins. "All this comes before baptism, independent of it, and in baptism finds an outward expression."[60] Within this context of salvation first and then baptism, Frost provides a significant illustration for this study. He speaks of a "young boy" reading through the first three chapters of the Gospel of John. Upon reading John 3:7, "the boy leaped to his feet, rushed into the house shouting as he came, 'O mother, mother, something has happened; something has happened.' That was the new birth; it was of God."[61] Within the context of this example of child conversion, Frost states, "then baptism." In light of this example, it is clear that for Frost, children are able cognitively to understand conversion. Further, when converted such children should be baptized. There is no support for the ideas of baptismal delay or the inability of children within Frost's theology.

Like Frost, O. C. S. Wallace, the Southern Baptist pastor of First Baptist Baltimore, emphasized obedience in relation to the timing of baptism. While Wallace fails to offer a specific age for baptism, he does emphasize that "the meaning of the ordinance suggests the priority of this duty."[62] For Wallace, baptism is then the first action a new believer takes after salvation. Therefore, there is no room for baptismal delay for Wallace.

George Truett, pastor of the First Baptist Church of Dallas, emphasizes the need for a child's salvation within the context of a sermon on the importance of training a child in the ways of the Lord.[63] He does this through asking his audience a question: "How can parents be comfortable and satisfied when the children are not anchored to our Savior and Lord?"[64] Next, Truett presents a testimony of a man who had pleaded and prayed with his son "to come to Christ." Truett goes on to explain how the prayer was answered. "It was just one week [from the time the prayers were offered] until I baptized that boy in this baptistery, upon profession of the boy's faith in Christ."[65] Truett, then, believes that parents should worry about the salvation of their young children. Parents should pray for their children's salvation not in an abstract sense, but with a sense of urgency. Upon salvation, Truett's example shows that he made every effort to baptize children quickly.

One of the most comprehensive statements on the baptism of children during this era of Baptist life comes from Baptist pastor Joshua Wills in his *Believer's Manual on Baptism*. Therein, he argues that parents and churches, while not having an obligation to baptize children, do have an obligation "to train up children in the 'nurture and admonition of the Lord.'"[66] Building upon this idea, Wills further points out that children, can accept the blessed truth which parents affectionately inculcate, and [as a result] many instances of early piety have occurred in every age, and genuine conversions occur among children of tender years [as] the direct result of parental instructions….Hence the duty of every parent to children is not primarily baptism, but training and instructing them in order to their nurture in the Lord, enabling them in the exercise of faith to understand; they believe on the Lord Jesus, which is the prerequisite for baptism, not reversing "the order of the day,"…it is well to observe the New Testament teaching: first train, then the child will believe, and upon their confession of the Lord Jesus administer the ordinance of baptism.[67]

Willis, then, emphasizes the temporal priority of conversion over baptism against paedobaptist practices. Yet, even while encouraging Baptists parents to make sure that their children are converted, Willis notes that once they believe, baptize.

A final well-known Southern Baptist voice from this era is that of New Testament scholar A. T. Robertson. Within his treatment of the doctrine of baptism, there is a brief but powerful note relevant to this study within his criticism of the evangelical paedobaptism. Therein, he states that paedobaptists "lay more stress upon baptism than Baptist do, since they will not wait till the child is converted."[68] He goes on, stating that paedobaptism is "a relic of fears that infants would perish unless they were baptized."⁶⁹ Robertson argues that conversion is the prerequisite for baptism. Conversely for Robertson, once the child is converted, then baptize. Additionally, there is a note of caution in Robertson's exhortation, specifically parents who urge baptism for their unconverted young children should be reminded that their young child will not perish if they are not baptized.

During the first half of the twentieth century, direct treatments of the relation of children to conversion or baptism remained uncommon. What can be known of the views of leading Baptists at this time is largely known through inference. Mullins indirectly argues that children are incapable of conversion prior to the age of 12. Frost argues that any regenerated person has an obligation to be baptized and notes that young children can be converted. Truett and Wills believe children are valid candidates for baptism while in contrast Robertson cautions patience, waiting for the child to be ready to be converted. Still, once converted, children should be baptized for Robertson. Based on this evidence, it follows that while some Baptists may have practiced baptismal delay or counseled that children did not need to be converted, none of the surveyed individuals goes so far as to explicitly argue for such limits or to insist that such limits should be rigid. In contrast, other Baptists assume that even young children are valid candidates for conversion and baptism

Conclusions

As a result of this study, threee conclusions can be drawn about Southern Baptists and their views of children. First, early Southern Baptist expressed a greater openness to the conversion and baptism of children than has previously been noted. Specifically, Fuller, Broadus, Dagg, Manly Jr., Strong, and Hiscox all imply or argue that children can be converted. Fuller and Dagg go even further in directly arguing for their baptism and church membership.

Second, the idea that children can be converted and should be baptized is not new for Southern Baptists. This idea has strong historical support within the context of the Southern Baptist Convention. Therefore, the myth of a historically uniform practice regarding child baptisms among Southern Baptists is to be rejected.

Third, the first notable Southern Baptists to imply children are cognitively incapable of conversion and baptism until reaching a specific age was E. Y. Mullins. The idea that children are not cognitively capable of being converted, baptized, or functioning as church members is not found in the vast majority of nineteenth and early twentieth century Southern Baptist literature.

Endnotes

[1] This article is drawn in part from Chapter 3 of Robert Matz, "Should Southern Baptists Baptize Their Children? A Biblical, Historical, Theological Defense of the Consistency of the Baptism of Young Children with Credobaptistic Practices" (PhD diss., Liberty University, 2015).

[2] For example, Mark Dever makes this argument stating that "This practice of delaying for maturity—similar to other delays commanded in Scripture (e.g., marriage, responsibility in OT Israel, service in the army in the OT... was formerly common in the United States. Baptisms of children eight or nine years of age, or even younger, were either unheard of or very rare." Mark Dever, "Baptism in the Context of the Local Church," in *Believer's Baptism: Sign of the New Covenant in Christ*, ed. Thomas R. Schreiner and Shawn D. Wright, NAC Studies in Bible & Theology 2 (Nashville, TN: B & H Academic, 2006), 346.

[3] This claim originates with Samuel Southard who argued that "there has been a steady drop in the chronological age at which churches will accept a child's accountability for sin." Gary Deane in his dissertation from SWBTS made a similar claim stating "there has been a growing tendency of children to profess a religious conversion in Baptist churches at a continuously earlier age." Both substantiated their claims through late nineteenth and early twentieth century studies from Starbuck, Coe, Hall, Althearn, and Clark. Samuel Southard, *Pastoral Evangelism* (Nashville, TN: Broadman, 1962), 86. Gary T. Deane, "An Investigation of the Child's Conception of Christian Conversion, Baptism, and Church Membership Compared with Jean Piaget's Stages of Cognitive Development" (EdD diss., Southwestern Baptist Theological Seminary, 1982), 6-7. Edwin Starbuck, *The Psychology of Religion: An Empirical Study of the Growth of Religious Consciousness* (London: Walter Scott, 1899), 33ff. George Albert Coe, *The Psychology of Religion* (Chicago, IL: The University of Chicago Press, 1916), 152-74; idem, *The Spiritual Life: Studies in the Science of Religion* (London: Fleming H. Revell, 1914), 29-55. G. Stanley Hall, *Adolescence: Its Psychology and Its Relations to Physiology, Anthropology, Sociology, Sex, Crime, Religion and Education* (Charlottesville, VA: D. Appleton, 1905), 2:290. Walter S. Althearn et al., *The Indiana Survey of Religious Education: The Religious Education of Protes-*

tants in an American Commonwealth (New York, NY: George H. Doran, 1922-1924), 2:388-92. Elmer T. Clark, *The Psychology of Religious Awakening* (New York, NY: MacMillan, 1929), 116. See also Paul E. Johnson, *Psychology of Religion* (Nashville, TN: Abingdon, 1955), 127.

[4] Andy Addis, et al., *Pastors' Task Force on SBC Evangelistic Impact* (Alpharetta, GA: Baptist Press, 2014), 1, accessed March 3, 2015, http://www.namb.net/baptismtaskforce/. Ed Stetzer, "Disturbing Trends in Baptisms," *Center for Missional Research Insights Newsletter*, October 10, 2006, http://www.namb.net/site/apps/nl/content2.asp?c=9qKILUOzEpH&b=2027651&ct=3198417/. Kevin P. Emmert, "Baptizing the Dora Generation: Why Preschooler Faith Is So Controversial," *Christianity Today*, June 10, 2014, 1, accessed March 7, 2014, http://www.christianitytoday.com/ct/2014/june-web-only/sbc-preschool-baptisms-under-age-6-southern-baptists.html.

[5] Dever offers this line of argument. He gives the age of baptism for a number of notable nineteenth century Baptists and notes how they were almost all baptized in late adolescences. Dever, "Baptism in the Local Church," 346 fn 24.

[6] The problems with applying the five studies mentioned in footnote 2 above to a Southern Baptist context are numerous. For example, Starbuck's study did not include data from Baptists and only provides specific data on persons between the age of 9 and 25 (despite him specifically stating elsewhere that he had respondents both above and below this age range). Coe's study also does not deal with Baptists, as he simply takes Starbuck's data and combines it with the data of a second study on conversions in mystical religions. Hall also did not sample Baptists, instead surveying Methodist-Episcopal ministers, alumni of a Methodist school and YMCA members. Altherean's study did not directly measure conversion ages and instead looked at Sunday School practices in Indiana in the 1920s (a state outside of Southern Baptist's regional influence during that era). In contrast to the other four studies, Clark's did sample Baptists. Yet he only sampled college students. In so doing, he excluded both late in life converts and the uneducated (of whom a vast majority of Southern Baptists were in this era). Starbuck, *Psychology of Religion*, 28, 30-34. George Albert Coe, *The Psychology of Religion*, 152-74; idem, *The Spiritual Life*, 29-55. Hall, *Adolescence*, 2:290. Clark, *Religious Awakening*, 27-28. For a more thorough treatment of these issues see Matz, "Should Southern Baptist Baptize Their Children?", 134-136, 143-147.

[7] The claim of rising preschool baptisms exists within the context of the data from the Annual Church Profile. This profile shows that the total number of preschool aged baptisms has fallen between a low 1,146 in 1966 to a high of 4,574 baptisms in 1999. As a percentage of all baptisms, preschool baptisms have made up between 0.32% of all baptisms to 1.15% of all baptisms. In comparison to the other categories surveyed, the other categories have between 4 and 50 times more baptisms each year than there are preschool baptisms. Thus the significance of rising rates of preschool baptism is overstated. The number of baptisms broken down by age group was given to the au-

thor by Paula Hancock of Lifeway Christian Resources. Paula Hancock, email message to author, June 13, 2014.

[8] During the first half of the last decade, the number of preschool baptisms leveled off, fluctuating between 4,403 baptisms (2000) and 4,139 baptisms (2003). From 2005 through 2010, the number of preschool baptism dropped significantly. In 2005, there were 4,272 preschool aged baptisms. By 2010, there were 3,356. This was the lowest total for under-six baptisms since 1995. As a percentage of total baptisms, baptisms of children under the age of six peaked in 2005 at 1.15% of all baptisms. From 2005 to 2010, under-six baptism fell to 1.01% of all baptisms, its lowest percentage since 1997.

[9] Dever's research in collecting baptismal ages is impressive. Still, offering this list as evidence that the practice of young baptism is novel fails as this list is largely anecdotal. Southern Baptists baptized millions of people over the course of their early history. To assert that Baptists in America as a whole rarely to never baptized young children because a list of select early Baptists figures were baptized at a later age, ignores the fact that a select list of leaders does not make up the whole of denominational life. Indeed, an article appearing on the online "Southern Baptist News and Analysis" website, *SBCToday*, by Dr. Tim Barnette has provided an alternative list noting the young age of conversion of several significant historical Baptist figures. Dever, "Baptism in the Context of the Local Church," 345. Tim Barnette, "About Baptizing Children," *SBCToday* March 3, 2015, accessed March 24, 2015, http://sbctoday.com/about-baptizing-children-dr-tim-barnette/#.

[10] There have been previous studies examining the views of Baptist's children and baptism globally, but no such study from a specifically Southern Baptist perspective. For other studies on the topic see Hugh Wamble, "Historic Practices Regarding Children," in *Children and Conversion*, ed. Clifford Ingle, (Nashville, TN: Broadman, 1970), 71-83. Leon McBeth, *A Sourcebook for Baptist Heritage* (Nashville, TN.: Broadman Press, 1990), 382-86. David F. Tennant, *Children in the Church: A Baptist View* (London: Baptist Publications, 1978), 3-37.

[11] The American Baptist Publication Society produced several works during the first part of the nineteenth century that touched on the topic of the baptism of children. Unfortunately, most of these works were not from a Southern perspective. Still, three works are of particular note as they note the variety of views regarding child baptism being disseminated among early American Baptists. First, from a Northern Baptist perspective, Wilson Jewell, a medical doctor from Philadelphia, offered a narrative on conversion and baptism of children. Written from a reformed perspective, Jewell defends believer's baptism in the context of a child who wants to come to faith in Christ, but is waiting for God's invading work. Although not explicit, Jewell implies that a child first becomes awakened to such desires around the age of eleven, but that such desires do not take full hold until at the earliest around the age of fourteen. Second, one of the founders of the Baptist movement in Sweden, Anders Wiberg, lived in New York for a few years. While there, he partnered with the publication society and wrote *Christian*

Baptism. In that text, Wiberg notes that "It is by no means uncommon for Baptist missionaries and preachers to actually baptize whole households, as may be abundantly seen in the journals of the denomination." He clarifies these households do not contain children "incapable of attaining to a perception of faith by means of instruction." Later, Wiberg clarifies his view of children noting that when early church text refer to the baptism of children they "ought to be understood as referring to the baptism of children of sufficient age to be conscious moral agents." Thus Wiberg distinguishes between children who are conscious moral agents and infants who are not. The former are fit for baptism, the later are not. Third, from a British perspective, the society offered R. Pengilly's *The Scripture Guide to Baptism* which implies that children are not cognitively capable of being converted (although he does not see a distinction between children and infants). Wilson Jewell, *The Baptism or the Little Inquirer: Designed for the Use of Sabbath Schools* (Philadelphia, PA: American Baptist Publication Society, 1835), 9,8-90. Anders Wiberg, *Christian Baptism: Set Forth in the Words of the Bible* (Philadelphia, PA: American Baptist Publication Society, n.d.), 103, 104, 244. R. Pengilly, *The Scripture Guide to Baptism: Containing a Faithful Citation of All the Passages of the New Testament Which Relate to This Ordinance*, 9th ed. (Philadelphia, PA: Baptist General Tract Society, 1837), 90-91.

[12] Hugh Wamble, "Historic Practices Regarding Children," in *Children and Conversion*, ed. Clifford Ingle, (Nashville, TN: Broadman, 1970), 82.

[13] For example, from a British perspective see Pengilly R., 90-91. See also Richard Fuller, *Baptism and the Terms of Communion* (1854; repr., Paris, AR: The Baptist Standard Bearer, Inc, 2006), 138-139. See also the discussion on Hiscox in the 1850-1900 section below.

[14] Charleston Baptist Association, *A Summary of Church Discipline: Shewing the Qualifications and Duties of the Officers and Members of a Gospel Church* (Charleston, SC: Markland, M'Iver, & Company, 1794), 122-25, accessed March 3, 2015, http://founders.org/library/index-5-2/charles/.

[15] Wamble, "Historic Practices Regarding Children," 82.

[16] Isaac Taylor Hinton, *The History of Baptism: Both from the Inspired and Uninspired Writings* (Philadelphia, PA: American Baptist Publication and S.S. Society, 1840), 102.

[17] Hinton, *History of Baptism*, 102.

[18] The dates of these early Baptist range from the 1760s to 1800, as noted in Joe M. King, *History of South Carolina Baptist* (Columbia, SC: R. L. Bryan, 1964), 148.

[19] O. W. Taylor, *Early Tennessee Baptists 1769-1832* (Nashville, TN: Executive Board of the Tennessee Baptist Convention, 1957), 89.

[20] McBeth, *A Sourcebook for Baptist Heritage*, 291, 384.

[21] Northern Baptist Theologian Augustus Strong, whose systemtatic theology was widely used in the South also wrote on the issue of child baptisms. He affirmed the baptism of children. In an 1865 sermon, Strong argues that "the age of possible conversion

begins from the first moment of moral consciousness," which varies from child to child with for some it being "five, seven, ten or twelve. If he is old enough to sin consciously and deliberately, he is old enough to be an assured partaker in the benefits of Christ's salvation." He continues, noting that "the natural possibilities for good are greatest at the moment of first unfolding of moral consciousness and are less every moment thereafter." Therefore, he argues that it is imperative for parents to disciple their children from their earliest days. As soon as children come to faith "but as soon as the child claims credible evidence of such faith, his right to admission to Christ's church is indisputable." In response to arguments that Scripture is silent as to the conversion of children, he notes the early piety of Joseph, Samuel, Abijah, Josiah, Daniel, John the Baptist, and Timothy. Clearly, Strong believes children are valid candidates for conversion and baptism. Augustus Strong, "The Conversion of Children," *The Watchman Examiner* (September 23, 1965): 584-85.

[22] McBeth, *The Baptist Heritage*, 386-391.

[23] Richard Fuller, *Baptism, and the Terms of Communion: an Argument*, The Baptist Distinctives Series 9, 3rd ed. (1854; repr., Paris, AR: Baptist Standard Bearer, 2006), 112.

[24] Ibid., 139.

[25] Ibid., 109.

[26] Ibid., 117.

[27] Emphasis mine John Broadus, *The Duty of Baptists to Teach Their Distinctive Views*, (1880; repr., Seattle, WA: Amazon Digital Services, 2011), Kindle, location 54-57.

[28] Emphasis mine. John L. Dagg, *A Manual of Church Order* (Nashville, TN: Southern Baptist Publication Society, 1858), 145.

[29] Basil Manly, Jr. *Little Lessons for Little People* (Charleston, SC: Southern Baptist Publication Society, 1858, 2) as cited in f, *A Sourcebook for Baptist Heritage*, 293.

[30] Manly Jr, *Little Children*, 2 as cited in McBeth, *Sourcebook*, 293.

[31] Ibid.

[32] James Petigru Boyce, *Abstract of Systematic Theology* (Philadelphia, PA: American Baptist Publication Society, 1889), 11.

[33] Ibid., 12.

[34] Ibid., Appendix A.

[35] J. R Graves, *The Relation of Baptism to Salvation* (Texarkana, TX: Baptist Sunday School Committee, 1881), 41.

[36] Ibid., 43.

[37] J. R Graves, *Christian Baptism* (Texarkana, TX: Baptist Sunday School Committee, 1881), 35.

[38] Ibid., 36.

[39] Graves, *The Relation of Baptism to Salvation*, 44.

[40] Ibid.

[41] B. H. Carroll, *Defending the Faith and Practice of Baptist*, comp. J. W. Crowder (Fort Worth, TX: Southwestern Baptist Seminary, 1957), 75-76.

[42] B. H. Carroll, *The Ten Dollar Gold Piece and the Baptized Boy*, comp. J. W. Crowder (Fort Worth, TX: Southwestern Baptist Seminary, 1957), 104-107.

[43] Edward Hiscox, *The Standard Manual for Baptist Churches* (Philadelphia, PA: American Baptist Publication Society, 1903), 137-38.

[44] Determining the age Hiscox has in view for children is particularly challenging. In his discussion of the historical rise of paedobaptism, he uses the terms infant and child interchangeably. Therein, he notes a quote from Tertullian about the rise of infant baptism in the early third century A.D. as the first possible allusion to its practice. Such was lamentable for Tertullian, from whom Hiscox argues that infant baptism was at best rare at the start of the third century and was thus a historical innovation. Yet, Hiscox then shifts his focus regarding Tertullian's quote and calls into question if Tertullian had actual infant in view in his baptismal lament. He states, "When the baptism of children began, it was not that of unconscious infants at all, as is now practiced, but, as Bunsen declares, of 'little growing children, from six to ten years old.'" It is unclear whether Hiscox views the baptism of six to ten year olds that potentially originates in Tertullian's day as an acceptable practice or not. Still, such children are contrasted by Hiscox with "unconscious infants" indicating that Hiscox views children as young as six as self-aware and thus potentially as appropriate candidates for conversion and baptism. Hiscox, *The Standard Manual*, 132-33.

[45] H. R McClendon, *The Bible on Baptism* (Louisville, KY: Baptist Book Concern, 1896), 297.

[46] Hammett substantiates this by claiming that delaying the baptism of children until late adolescences at the earliest was common amongst the early Anabaptists and by noting the pattern of eighteenth century Baptists church to strongly question those churches in their association that baptized anyone prior to late adolescences. While both of these claims lie outside the scope of this paper, they do provide an area for additional historical research regarding the baptismal practices of children by subsequent scholars. John S. Hammett, *Biblical Foundations for Baptist Churches: A Contemporary Ecclesiology* (Grand Rapids, MI: Kregel, 2005), 272.

[47] See McBeth, *The Baptist Heritage*, Chapter 15.

[48] They stated, "Christian baptism is the immersion of a believer in water in the name of the Father, the Son, and the Holy Spirit. The act is a symbol of our faith in a crucified, buried and risen Savior. It is prerequisite to the privileges of a church relation..."

[49] See Malcolm Yarnell, "Changing Baptist Understandings of the Royal Priesthood," in *The Rise of the Laity in Evangelical Protestantism*, ed. Deryck W. Lovegrove (London: Routledge, 2002), 236-52.

[50] They "insist that man's action is not required by God's grace. Irresistible grace will sweep the elect into the kingdom without co-operation on their part. This, of course, simply ignores human freedom. Infant baptism also assumes that grace operates without the co-operation of the will of the child, but with a striking difference. In the one case it is insisted that we must not intermeddle with God's plans of persuading sinners to believe, while in the other it is urged that we must intermeddle and assist God's decree by bringing the infant to the baptismal font."

[51] Horace Bushnell, *Christian Nurture* (1861; repr., Grand Rapids, MI: Baker, 1979).

[52] Mullins, *Axioms*, 175.

[53] Ibid., 177.

[54] Ibid, 178.

[55] Mullins's language here is problematic. While Jesus clearly learned and grew in both wisdom and stature with God and man (Luke 2:52), Mullins's assumption that this is Jesus' first encounter with the Jewish system or that he was only at this age able to grasp the significance of the Jewish system go significantly beyond what the text actually says (Luke 2:41-52). Further, Mullins's language about Jesus' "sensitive soul" is at best sentimentalism. Ibid., 182.

[56] Ibid., 182-83.

[57] J. M. Frost, *The Moral Dignity of Baptism* (Nashville, TN: Sunday School Board of the Southern Baptist Convention, 1905), 64-65.

[58] J. M Frost, *Evangelism and Baptism* (Nashville, TN: Baptist Sunday School Board, 1916), 41.

[59] Ibid., 45.

[60] Ibid., 64-66, 67.

[61] Ibid., 64-65.

[62] O. C. S Wallace, *What Baptist Believe* (Nashville, TN: Baptist Sunday School Board, c. 1913), 155-56.

[63] George Truett, *The Highest Welfare of the Home, 20 Centuries of Great Preaching*, vol. 8, ed. Clyde E. Fant and William M. Pinson (Waco, TX: Word, 1971), 168.

[64] Ibid., 170.

[65] Ibid., 171.

[66] Joshua E. Wills, *Believer's Manual on Baptism* (Philadelphia, PA: American Baptist Publication Society, 1910), 94.

[67] Ibid., 96, 99.

[68] A. T. Robertson, The *Spiritual Interpretation of the Ordinances* in *The Best of A.T. Robertson*, comp. Timothy George and Denise George (1911; repr., Nashville, TN: Broadman and Holman, 1998), 210.

[69] Ibid., 210.

Author Biography

Dr. Robert Matz works at Midwestern Seminary where he has served in both academic and administrative roles. Dr. Matz teaches courses on Christian Doctrine, Theology, Preaching, Apologetics, Church History and Ecclesiology. Administratively he serves as Director of Midwestern's undergraduate online program.

Family, Love, and Duty in Narnia

John F. McCard

And he answered them, "Who are my mother and my brothers?" And looking about at those who sat around him, he said, "Here are my mother and my brothers! For whoever does the will of God, he is my brother and sister and mother" (Mark 3:33-35).

Those who love *The Chronicles of Narnia* usually encounter the stories in three distinct ways. First, we hear or read the stories as children reveling in the adventure, wishing we were in Narnia but sometimes missing the Christian subtext. Second as we grow older, adults will often return to the stories and what themes may have once been *seen through a glass darkly* are now more clearly appreciated as C. S. Lewis' moral vision comes into focus. Finally, as parents, we return to the stories and hope that the virtues of love, courage, and duty will be imparted to our own children as they hear of the great lion, Aslan, and the children; Peter, Susan, Lucy, and Edmund for the first time.

Yet there is no denying that to ponder the lessons of the stories, they must be seen in the context of the Christian Gospels' own reflections on the duties and obligations of family. Therefore, I want to begin by offering a few reflections on the Gospel pericope from Mark. Not being a New Testament scholar, I realize I am sailing into uncharted waters. However, before turning to C. S. Lewis, Narnia, and Lewis' portrayal of familial relationships, I want to put this passage into a context for my reading of *The Chronicles of Narnia*.

Setting the framework for this discussion involves a careful examination of the way scholars have chosen to interpret the stories. So in the second section of the paper, I want to offer some reflections on the ways the Chronicles have traditionally and untraditionally been interpreted. To read any commentary on the Chronicles is to encounter writers like Philip Pullman (*His Dark Materials*), who believe they are the most pernicious books ever written, but there are also others like Anglican theologian, Rowan Williams who present a more balanced assessment:

> I am not out to decode images or to uncover a system; but I do hope to show how certain central themes hang together – a concern to do justice to the difference of God, the disturbing and exhilarating otherness of what we encounter in the life of faith; a relentless insistence on self-questioning, not so as to understand ourselves in the abstract or as "interesting" individuals, but simply to discover where we are afraid of the truth and where we turn away into self-serving falsehood; a passion to communicate the excess of joy that is promised by the truth of God in Christ. (Williams, 2012, p.7)

In the third and final section, I want to look at the way Lewis' vision of family and familial relationships are incarnated (or realized) in the Narnia stories. While I may not have time for an exhaustive study of all the familial relationships in the stories (that will have to wait for a dissertation), I want to examine a few incidences in Narnia and offer some tentative reflections on Lewis' social and ethical vision for familial relationships as they relate to the obedience one is called to give to Aslan and to Aslan alone.

Part One: Family Values in the First Century

While the gospel pericope from Mark seems to offer a redefinition of familial relationships, it is critical to remember the reason for Jesus' family showing up in the first place. They do not come to listen to Jesus' teaching or to marvel at His abilities as a healer. Instead His immediate family thinks He is *out of His mind*. The Greek suggests that Jesus' family shows up to take charge of Him in a way that suggests carrying Him off until He comes to His senses.

This encounter takes place in chapter three around the events of Jesus calling His twelve disciples, His new family together on the mountain. (Although in seeking the perfect family unit, Jesus did pick at least one bad apple.) There is also the intriguing account of the religious authorities accusing Jesus of casting out spirits by Beelzebub, the prince of demons.

Jesus is accused of being part of a demonic family and that His power over evil spirits is demonically given. Jesus responds to this charge in the strongest possible terms using the familiar language of a house being divided against itself not being able to stand and later, saying that blasphemy against the Holy Spirit is the one sin that will never be forgiven in the life to come.

These three events taken together, underscore that the author of the gospel is arguing that Jesus as the One who calls together this new family and the spirit that unites it cannot be demonically inspired. More importantly for our purposes this new family of followers/disciples cannot be confined to the familial (or tribal) relationships that have traditionally defined the children of Israel.

After making these statements Jesus turns His attention back to His biological family who are waiting outside the building and wish to take Him away from His new family who are on the inside. This return focus on family at the end of the chapter should not be surprising. Jesus has called together a new family in His twelve apostles. He has reminded His disciples that Satan cannot cast out Satan. And it is Jesus, in fact, who has taken charge of the world and the way Israel now should understand familial bonds and relationships.

This centering of "new familial relationships" is particularly significant in the late first and second centuries of the church's history. This was a time when Christians found themselves increasingly cast out of their traditional social and family groups. The pericope from Mark must have been comforting for alienated believers to hear. *"For whoever does the will of God, he is my brother and sister and mother."*

In one verse, Jesus tells His followers that relationships in the kingdom are no longer to be based on the bonds of blood kinship but, God's family is expanded to include all those who hunger for a relationship with God and are willing to do God's will as part of the new community of faith. Being born into a family (or part of the tribe of Israel) no longer offers the assurance of salvation or election as God's chosen people.

But before one is tempted to follow this pericope down a path, which suggests a complete redefinition of the term family, we should remember that even Jesus' new family, His disciples, were often no better at getting their priorities or their relationships right. They argued about who was greatest, and the two sons of thunder even used their mother to ask for positions of power and influence at Jesus' right and left hand.

Jesus instructs His followers that despite their imperfections they should work together to fulfill the will of God. This doing of God's will in fellowship together is what it means to be a "new family" in Mark's Gospel. This places one's membership in the family on an ethical foundation. Membership in a family is to be defined by what one does, not on who one is, or to whom they may be related. As David Garland writes:

> Jesus' response to the visit from his family would have been a shocker because it runs counter to the received wisdom of the age. The family was the basis of social and economic life and the source of one's identity. In the first century Mediterranean world, an individual's identity was basically that of a member of a group (dyadic personal identity). The genealogies and laws relating to family life in the Scriptures show the importance of membership in a family or clan (and village). In the Old Testament "life" is used almost interchangeably with "family." One's family was one's life, and to reject family or to be cast out of the family was to lose one's life. (1998, p. 131)

Christians in the early centuries of the church's existence understood that to follow Jesus was to lose the life they had once known, for a life of obedience to a reborn version of family in God's newly created kingdom. This verse, while shocking to modern ears, was at once comforting and reassuring to those who had been cast out. Jesus as the incarnated Word of God, the Word made flesh, is the One who has accepted and welcomed new members into God's family and given them new life even if they were tax collectors, prostitutes, or that pesky Syro-phonecian woman.

For our modern age, the verse can appear problematic especially when some are tempted to use this verse to set aside the moral and ethical scope of New Testament teaching on marriage and family. In the rush of some to redefine traditional roles within the family, Garland offers the following warning. Despite this expansion of the idea of family, Jesus fiercely condemned those who dodged parental responsibilities through legal technicalities (Mark 7:6-13), His dispatch of the healed Gerasense demonic back to his family (5:18-19) and His condemnation of divorce with the stern reminder (10:1-12) that it was because of humanity's sin that divorce was allowed and that Genesis sets up the proper context for marriage. In the beginning God made them male and female and that the two will indeed become one in holy marriage, fulfilling God's purpose for God's created world order (Garland, 1998, p.140). So one must be careful to imply that this verse means traditional bonds or duties to one's family are not important to Jesus or they can be changed to suit our own post-modern context.

What Jesus appears to be arguing for, is a more radical notion of obligation. This type of obedience or obligation to God is meant to prevent human beings from making our family or personal relationships an object of worship. Jesus after all did place the love of God before the love of neighbor.

N.T. Wright's assessment of this passage in his informal commentary, *Mark for Everyone*, criticizes the way that some relationships (within a family) can be placed on an altar of worship. He writes:

> ...In Jesus's world it was scandalous—as it would be in some places. The family bond was tight and long lasting. As with many non-Western cultures today, it was normal for children to live close to their parents, maybe even in the same house. The family unit would often be a business unit as well, sharing everything in common. What's more, for Jews, the close family bond was part of the God given fabric of thinking and living. Loyalty to the family was the local and specific outworking of loyalty to Israel as the people of God.....He (Jesus) slices through the whole traditional structure in one clean cut. He has a different vocation, a different mission, and it involves breaking hallowed family ties. God is doing the unthinkable: he is starting a new family, a new holy people, and is doing so without regard for ordinary human family bonds. (Wright, 2004, pp. 39-40)

For Wright, Jesus' words are meant to shake humanity out of its complacency and the self-satisfied nature of Israel's status as "a chosen people" in the first century. For Wright in the present age, our own Western Individualism is the guilty culprit. He writes,

> "How easy it is to slide back again into a sense of belonging, of group identity, that comes from something other than loyalty to Jesus. We substitute long standing friendship, membership in the same group, tribe, family, club, party, social class or whatever it may be. But the call to be 'around' Jesus, to listen to him, even if 'those outside' think us crazy, is what matters. The church in every generation, and in every place, needs to remember this and act on it." (Wright, 2004, p. 40).

Jesus' words are an antidote to the self-worship that can potentially corrupt the relationships humanity has with God. Jesus' redefinition is a reordering of human priorities. There is an innate human desire to set other relationships and other temporal things above or next to God when it comes to our worship or adoration.

But just as Jesus' words in Mark are designed to shake humanity out of its stupor and idolatry, Lewis reminds us in the Narnia stories that *Aslan is not a safe lion*. To encounter Aslan is to encounter the radical goodness that changes the nature of all human relationships. And to understand anew that with obedience to Aslan comes an expansion of our family and those human beings who are considered to be our brothers, sisters, and mothers.

Lewis argues that when it comes to human relationships, whether they are in Narnia or in the dreamlike world of *The Great Divorce*, there are still only two types of people that inhabit our world.

> There are only two kinds of people in the end: those who say to God, "Thy will be done," and those to whom God says, in the end, "Thy will be done." All that are in Hell, choose it. Without that self-choice there could be no Hell. No soul that seriously and constantly desires joy will ever miss it. (Lewis, 2001, p. 75)

In *The Great Divorce*, Lewis deftly describes the difference between relationships that are founded upon a good that is eternal and a good that is corrupted or marred by human sin. Relationships are corrupted time and time again in this story as men and women devour themselves and others and then look to God first for the transformation of imperfect relationships formed by their familial bonds and marital vows.

Additionally, there is another statement from *The Great Divorce* that undergirds the Narnian worldview. This theme is critical when it comes to understanding the difference between the permanency of the life to come and the false gods of familial relationship that many people are tempted to worship. "There is but one good; that is God. Everything else is good when it looks to Him and bad when it turns from Him" (Lewis, 2001, p. 106). This is the theme of obedience to Aslan that shapes many of the Narnian narratives.

Lewis consistently reinforces this when it comes to the ethical and social vision of human relationships that inform his Narnian vision. Whether it is Turkish delight or the dragonish thoughts of Eustace as he contemplates murder and revenge, each character and each relationship within Narnia is good as long as Aslan is placed in the preeminent position of authority and obedience. It goes bad when Aslan is ignored or the characters satisfy their own selfish desires.

This is not a theme that is only good for a magical land. It also applies to the relationships of father, mother, sister, brother, son, and daughter. For it is precisely those relationships within God's family that teach us how to live fully human lives as part of God's creation. The virtues of love, sacrifice, duty, and honor are part of what human beings learn when they understand the proper ordering of their loves and their desires. Lewis reminds his readers through his Narnian stories that none of these relationships are good in and of themselves.

As Gilbert Meilaender writes in his book on Lewis, *The Taste for the Other*, the point of human life is to live a certain dialectic between enjoyment and renunciation that is described as "'the sweet poison of the false infinite.' … Human beings have been created in a world of things [and relationships]; created to delight in things but never to seek security in them. That vision is captured by Lewis in imaginative worlds, and that task is defined by him in terms of the Christian story" (Meilaender, 1978, p. 44). It is to those stories and their interpretations we now turn.

Part Two: Narnia and Its Interpretations

It will come as no surprise to anyone that C. S. Lewis loved fairy tales and children's stories. He has remarked that a good story transcends age and time. What is read and enjoyed as a child should also be read and enjoyed as an adult or for Lewis the story is not worth reading.

He returned to his favorite stories throughout his life and the week that he died wrote to a friend that was rereading *The Illiad* and "enjoying it more than I ever did." His love of fairy tale stories though, is curious when it comes to how one defines the Narnia stories. While various interpretations for these stories have been offered through the years, perhaps one of the most interesting is Michael Ward's interpretation using medieval cosmology and identifying each book as one of the seven planets.

Peter Schakel interprets the Narnia Chronicles as fairy tales while others explain the philosophical underpinning of the stories as vehicles for moral and ethical teaching. As Paul Ford has written, "The Chronicles can be seen as Lewis' seven volume Magician's Book written to disenchant children of all ages of that Lewis found illusory and to re-enchant them by way of baptism of the imagination, all the things that really matter" (Ford, 1980, p. 2).

In this sense, they are understood as stories that impart objective moral truth to their students. In this way, they echo Lewis' themes in *The Abolition of Man* when he argues against the divorce of objective truth from human feelings. And the dangers of reducing moral truth (and for the Narnia stories human relationships) to a subjectivity based upon one's feelings or what one can personally gain through a relationship. Mr. Tumnus could have turned Lucy over to the White Witch, but he knew instinctively that this action was wrong in an objective sense. If he had acted solely on his feelings, his fear might have led him to betray his friend.

To read *The Chronicles of Narnia* is also to enter a magical world of talking animals, wicked witches, and heroic princes and princesses. However, there is one interesting difference in the Chronicles from traditional fairy tales. The children that visit these lands particularly in the first story, *The Lion, the Witch and the Wardrobe* do not finish their tale with happy marriages or raising families.

The kings and queens enjoy long reigns, but there are no apparent marriages or children that on a practical side would have provided heirs for their Narnian kingdom. While this may have made practical sense, family life would certainly have interfered with Peter, Susan, Lucy, and Edmund returning back to their own world, with the moral lessons they have learned. Does this narrative decision mean that Lewis did not believe in a traditional fairy-tale *happily ever after*? It depends on how a *happy ending* is defined. All of the stories end with the defeat of evil and the restoration of harmony to the land of Narnia and the return of the proper ordering of human relationships. But temporal human happiness can be a two-edged sword. As Gilbert Meilaender writes, "Lewis firmly believes that God will make us happy—indeed, that we cannot be happy apart from God. But he never says, 'Believe in God: he'll make you happy and you'll live the abundant life" (Meilaender, 1978, p. viii).

This theme runs through the various stories as Aslan sacrifices his life for Edmund and various other characters come to know the painful experiences that result from their own sacrifices for one another. They are called upon to put their allegiance to Aslan above their own inordinate desires. While this path is not always easy, it consistently proves to be the one they should follow. This can be seen in *Prince Caspian* when Aslan tells Lucy that she should have followed him, even if her brothers and sisters had refused to go along with her. Leaving *her family* for Aslan is a sacrifice that Lewis believes is worth making and the basis of all good ethical action that must look to Aslan first.

It is intriguing that happiness is often apart from the usual confines that one sees in familial or marital relationships. In fact, one of my critical arguments is that while Lewis uses the fairy tale form, he refuses simply to chart a course for us that makes it easy for the reader to default into a *marriage and happily ever after* mentality.

What is present in the Chronicles instead is that reordering of priorities in each of the character's lives and the assurance that what is given is not to be based on loyalty to one another, but loyalty first to Aslan as the basis for all human relationships. To say that Narnia is indeed a land of tradition and value, but not necessarily in the way that we may have supposed and not at the expense of the obedience that the characters must first have to Aslan.

In this way, echoing Tolkien's writings on Fairy Stories, The Chronicles contain within their structure three qualities that capture their appeal: Escape, Recovery, and Consolation. As Schakel writes:

Escape and Recovery lead into the ultimate value of fairy stories; the consolation afforded by a happy ending. "Ending" however, might not be the best word. Fairy stories, says Tolkien, have no true ending, but are always characterized by a "joyous 'turn,'" produced by a "sudden and miraculous grace." It is the nature of tragedy to result in a catastrophe; it is the nature of the fairy stories to end in what Tolkien named *Eucatastrophe*, the good catastrophe. "The *Eucatastrophic* tale is the true form of fairy-tale, and its highest function," he asserts. The presence of *Eucatastrophe* does not deny the existence of sorrow and failure. Rather, it denies universal final defeat and relates to what we said about desire. In its denial of defeat it offers a basis for hope and is an instance of *evangelium*, of good news, "giving a fleeting glimpse of Joy, Joy beyond the walls of the world" (Schakel, 2005, p. 30).

Aslan remains the central dominant figure of the stories and it is through him that characters come to knowledge of themselves and the tasks they have been set to accomplish. The moral truths they learn and the radical goodness of God (and Aslan) insure that they will come to know what it means to be a family in relationship with God and never apart from the demands that go along with their duties to one another as members of Aslan's family.

Part Three: Familial Relationships and Narnia

While I do not have the time to offer a comprehensive review of all familial relationships in the stories, I do want to offer several observations on the roles of fathers, mothers, and siblings in Narnia. These roles might incarnate Lewis' vision of what it means to live obediently as part of Aslan's family within the imaginary world that he has created.

In *The Lion, the Witch and the Wardrobe*, the parents of the four children send them away from London for their own safety. While the movie version fleshes out the familiar theme of dad being sent off to war, the original book largely passes over the role of the parents. We know little of them, except they cared about the safety of their children and made sure they would be safe from the London blitz. When the children are faced with a crisis, they end up consulting the professor who dispenses what may appear to be fatherly advice. However for the most part there are few adult figures that appear in a positive light.

For example, when Edmund first encounters the White Witch she offers to adopt him as the heir to her throne. His brother and sisters are an inconvenient afterthought, but a new ruler will need courtiers. So he agrees to betray them for the offer of power and Turkish delight. Edmund in a sense asks to sit on the right and left hand of the present ruler, but he does not realize that in forsaking the bonds of kinship he has allied himself to a demonic ruler and forsaken obedience to the one true ruler of the land.

The one positive domestic relationship that we are allowed to see in the stories is the one between Mr. and Mrs. Beaver, who present a picture of a happily married couple. When the children first arrive, Mr. and Beaver rescue them and invite them into their home for a delicious meal, warm hospitality, and stories about Aslan. This section of the story is one of comfort and security prior to the challenges that will come from the betrayal, the death, and the resurrection of Aslan.

In the next book, *Prince Caspian*, a thousand years have passed and the gentle world of Narnia has been turned upside down. Animals are in hiding and King Miraz rules the land, suppressing all elements of the old Narnia even sending an old nurse away who tried to tell stories to Caspian. However once again, we see the parental figure as dangerous. Once Miraz's son is born, he no longer needs Caspian and makes plans to kill him.

The only family Caspian has in the world is the very person he cannot depend upon to protect him. Instead, we see him turning to the old Narnians that are in hiding and embarking on a plot to return Narnia to the proper ordering of its original creation. The book ends with Caspian ascending the throne, with a stern reminder from Aslan that being a human is both a source of pride and of humility. Once again obedience to Aslan is the central element of the story that binds those relationship and duties together.

In the prequel to the previous stories, *The Magician's Nephew*, there are two intriguing familial relationships that drive the narrative. First there is Digory's uncle, dabbling in magic and using Digory and Polly to satisfy his own curiosity and lust for power. He tells Digory that ordinary rules do not apply to him, so he is free of the normal constraints that bind one person to another. Digory's uncle freely abandons his own duties to his nephew in his quest for power in his own world and any other world he may wish to conquer.

The primary relationship that undergirds the flow of the narrative is Digory's mother's illness and her potential death. As the story unfolds, he thinks of asking Aslan for something to cure his mother, but eventually goes on a quest to find an apple that will provide a magic tree to protect Narnia from the White Witch. Obedience to Aslan must come before the desires he has to see his mother made well.

While the journey to find the tree is easy, the difficult part comes when he is tempted by the White Witch to forsake his quest to cure his mother. She says to him:

> "But what about this mother of yours whom you pretend to love so?"
> "What's she got to do with it?" said Digory.
> "Do you not see, Fool, that one bite of that apple would heal her? You have it in your pocket. We are here by ourselves and the Lion is far away. Use your Magic and go back to your own world. A minute later you can be at your Mother's bedside, giving her the fruit." (Lewis, 2013, p. 64)

Digory is able to resist the temptation when the White Witch tells him to leave Polly behind, but he is still wounded by the choice he has made and torn by the conflicting duties and desires of his young life. Meilaender describes this "as the wound inflicted by grace on nature is a terrible one" (Meilaender, 1978, p. 137). As he writes:

> But it is also true that the natural love cannot come to its fruition apart from grace. Digory and Polly mention to Aslan that the Witch had already eaten one of the apples. They suppose, therefore, that Aslan must have made some mistake in thinking the Witch would be afraid of the tree and would stay away when it was planted in Narnia.

> "Child," he replied, "that is why all the rest are now a horror to her. That is what happens to those who pluck and eat fruits at the wrong time and in the wrong way. The fruit is good, but they loathe it ever after" (p.157)
> Aslan tells Digory that the fruit would certainly have healed his mother, but it would not, finally, have brought joy. "The day would come when both you and she would have looked back and said it would have been better to die in that illness" (p.158) (Meileander, 1978, p. 137)

This is what would have happened had Digory stolen the apple, but he learned what it means to be obedient to Aslan, and to embrace the life that comes from doing the will of God (Aslan). He is able to experience the restoration of his mother to health. She is healed by another apple eaten and enjoyed in the proper order and way. Perhaps the apple is eaten properly because the relationship between mother and son is now based on trust and not fear.

Conclusion

It might appear simplistic to say that the proper ordering of relationships begins with God first and love of neighbor second or in the Narnia stories the obedience one owes first to Aslan. Lewis also believed that the goods of family life, the relationships that human beings have within their family and circle of friends, must be enjoyed and used in the proper way. Always, with the understanding that love can, if human beings are not careful, claim a preeminent place of worship that would seek to replace God.

Lewis consistently reminds us in Narnia, that human beings are self-centered creatures who desire their own pleasure apart from the relationship with the one that would make the apple taste good and the Turkish delight truly delightful. In this way, Lewis reminds his readers that there is joy in the world, but only a joy (or happiness) that comes from the obedience and relationship one has with Aslan.

To experience the luxurious delights of the Narnian world is to know first the creator of that world, to hear the song of his creation and to give one's obedience and love to the one from whom all other joy and happiness is derived. This is the vision that Lewis would have us reflect upon as readers of his stories. It is not a redefinition or supplanting of family duties and sacrifices. Instead, Lewis seeks to teach his readers that to be a true brother, sister, or mother means that we first owe our allegiance and obedience to the one that made human goodness and happiness possible in our present world and in the life that is to come when we have left these Shadowlands.

References

Ford, Paul (1994). *The Companion to Narnia: A Complete Guide to the Magical World of C.S. Lewis's The Chronicles of Narnia.* San Francisco, CA: Harper Collins.

Garland, D. E. (1998). *The NIV Application Commentary: Mark.* Grand Rapids, MI: Zondervan.

Lewis, C. S. (2001). *The Great Divorce.* New York, NY: HarperCollins.

Lewis, C. S. (2013). *The Complete Chronicles of Narnia.* New York, NY: Harper Collins.

Meilaender, G. (1978). *The Taste for the Other: The Social and Ethical Thought of C. S. Lewis.* Grand Rapids, MI: William B. Eerdmans Publishing.

Schakel, P. J. (2005). *The Way into Narnia: A Readers Guide.* Grand Rapids, MI: William B. Eerdmans Publishing.

Williams, R. (2012). *The Lion's World: A Journey into the Heart of Narnia.* Oxford: Oxford University Press.

Wright, T. (2004). *Mark for Everyone.* London: Westminister John Knox Press.

Author Biography

John F. McCard is the Rector of St. Martin in the Fields Church in Atlanta. He holds a Doctor of Ministry Degree from Virginia Theological Seminary. Fr. John has taught classes and led workshops on C. S. Lewis at various churches and seminaries throughout the country.

Singles: Our Forgotten Families

Jackson Watts

Recently my wife asked me the following question: "Does a husband and wife count as a family even if they don't have children?" The question was more of a conversation starter than a typical question. She knew that a husband and a wife constituted a "household" in the New Testament sense of the word. Yet once the word "family" was introduced, somehow it felt like one had to strain a bit more to make our domestic arrangement conform to the mental picture of the family we had been conditioned to form.

Those who worship in evangelical churches—especially churches who embrace a D6 concept of family and ministry—are likely to give pause at her question. Most Christians do not come to their understanding of particular terms and ideas by searching the pages of Bible dictionaries, or even reliable sources like the Oxford English Dictionary. They arrive at their understanding by way of observation, as well as imbibing the background assumptions entailed in the preaching and teaching they hear each week. This is not to say that evangelical preaching is devoid of clearly defined explanations. Rather, it is simply to note that generally in the context of the local church certain cultural assumptions are at work, which function as boundary-markers for what is known (or thought to be known), and what is said or left unstated. Because many parachurch ministries and local churches operate from the assumption that a family is a mother, father, and at least one child, a certain picture of family life has largely defined the default thinking of many of those in the local church.

My argument is that this default picture, while not entirely false nor automatically harmful, is limited and detrimental to having a holistic ministry to a growing part of the evangelical church family: singles. Singles are, in many cases, our forgotten family members who must be biblically and practically understood if we hope to have healthy churches in a changing American landscape. Moreover, a proper account of singleness helps us better understand the Gospel, and it helps us develop a stronger culture of discipleship and service.

Terminological Problems: Defining Singleness

In a book about the ethics of animal treatment, ethicist Charles Camosy notes how our use of language can obscure some of the deeply moral dimensions of creaturely life. Specifically, by calling cows "beef" and pigs "pork" at the stage of consumption, we are disconnected "from the fact that we are eating the flesh of a nonhuman animal" (Camosy, 2013, p. 83). Similarly, by limiting the word "family" to refer only to homes where children are present, or using modifiers like "single-parent" before family, we begin to disconnect church households on the basis of their precise composition. While some distinction may indeed be relevant and helpful for some types of instruction, training, or service, this disconnect tends to influence other dimensions of church life whenever it grows out of a larger misunderstanding of the "other." For many churches, singles are the others.

One of the main practical problems of the church's vision of singleness is that it tends to be limited to seeing singles as younger, unmarried persons who are generally expected to be married at some point in the future. As we will see later, one of the latent problems with this perspective is that it ignores the potential value of singleness (that is, a life of celibacy) as seen in Scripture. A second problem is that whenever the single label is ascribed only to younger unmarried persons, it creates confusion among church leaders and single members themselves about where they belong in particular. A "College and Career" class or ministry is a safe haven for many singles trying to live through young adulthood without the expectations of imminent marriage constantly being imposed on them. However, at one point would a single person graduate from such a class? Moreover, what happens for the married member who unexpectedly loses a spouse, thus becoming a widow early in life? How would the presence of children in such a home alter one's self-understanding as a member in the body?

Terminological problems reflect and reinforce conceptual problems, and conceptual problems tend to reflect and reinforce practical problems.

Therefore, before proceeding to considering singleness in biblical perspective, we should keep in view a couple of clarifications with respect to terminology.

Singleness is to be understood in its normal linguistic sense as referring to any unmarried adult. They may be single by virtue of having never married, due to the death of a spouse, or due to divorce. We should additionally observe that none of these scenarios are fully indicative of a person's age. In other words, the never-married person, the widow/widower, or divorcee may be 25 years old or 85 years old. This simple, but important detail must shape how the church sees its entire single membership, along with their unique needs and opportunities with respect to the church's mission and ministry. "Single" is not a one-size-fits-all category that can be quickly understood without context or background.

Another important clarification concerns basic terms like chastity and celibacy. Chastity is to be understood as the full expression (especially in a physical sense) of spiritual purity in all of one's life, whether married or single. A chaste marriage is a couple solely devoted to one another in intimacy, never looking outside the marriage for such satisfaction. A chaste single is one who does not engage in sexual activity of any sort, whether premarital sex, pornography, or any other impure activity. Celibacy, on the other hand, is what is traditionally thought of as the gift of singleness, as alluded to in 1 Corinthians 7. It is not simply being in the state of chaste singleness, but it is rather a special spiritual gift or calling to *remain* unmarried and chaste.

My argument does not entirely hinge upon whether remaining celibate is to be understood as a spiritual gift (*charisma*) in the conventional sense of the word, a moral choice in view of a special divine call (which presumably would entail the gift), or a social circumstance in which God enables one to live faithfully for whatever period they happen to remain in it. However, there are two further considerations essential for this argument to stand: First, while a biblical study of the word "family" or "household" does in fact show that the assumption of marriage and children is not an unreasonable one, this does not negate the fact that the church itself is also said to be the family of God. In fact, it is our primary bond of loyalty in this life if we are to take the words of Christ seriously (Mark 3:32-35; Luke 14:26; John 19:26). Second, our increasingly complex contemporary ministry milieu will require us to have a stronger grasp on the spiritual and practical concerns that surround a biblical view of singleness.

The Challenge of Singleness in Contemporary Context

The church of Jesus Christ will never solely consist of well-adjusted, spiritually mature couples with children in the home. It will include single members who have not yet been married. It will include singles who may never marry. It will include singles who have been brought into a state of singleness through the tragedy of divorce or death of a spouse. Nearly one-half (102 million) of the American, adult population was single as of 2011. 62% of adults (18 years+) had never been married (*Unmarried and Single Americans Week, 2012*). In our well-intentioned efforts to focus on the family, is it possible that the increasing prevalence of singles should cause us to look closer at the church? Or, perhaps to recognize that one can have a more expansive view of the household (Greek *oikonomia*) to include single Christians without compromising on the biblical definition of marriage?

Given the church's historical record with respect to singleness, it is not surprising that many challenges are bound up with framing singleness as a spiritually significant way of life. Because celibacy as a morally superior choice—a predominant view for most of the Medieval period—seems to contradict the creational ethic that most Protestant theology has articulated, many have not spent time developing an actual theology of singleness. Moreover, the apostolic witness to how marriage uniquely bears witness to the Gospel (*e.g.* Ephesians 5:22-33) presents a positive vision of marriage, which makes it seem like the more spiritually substantive way of life for the church to spend time nurturing.

Aside from these factors, other cultural forces have actively contributed to the marginalization of singles in the evangelical church. Speaking of this marginalization, Köstenberger and Jones write, "Post-adolescent singles are probably the most overlooked social group in the contemporary Western church" (Köstenberger & Jones, 2010, p. 167). Part of this stems from the perception of singles as being unwilling to commit to a godly pursuit of courtship and marriage. Evangelical leaders such as Albert R. Mohler, Jr. of the Southern Baptist Theological Seminary have made such assertions. Significantly inflated cohabitation rates seem to substantiate the belief that singles not only have problem with sexual immorality, but problems with commitment. Anecdotally, Köstenberger and Jones (2010, p. 167) also observe that even among those single Christians still in good standing with the church, suspicions persist.

They note, when someone does remain single well into his or her twenties and thirties, either by choice or by circumstances, many people begin to try to diagnose the problem (be it sexual orientation, physical appearance, intellectual ability, social ineptitude, unduly high standards, or other factors) that has trapped the single person in the unnatural and undesirable condition of being unmarried. Such perceptions are more likely to abound whenever the church does not understand singleness as a divine gift or calling (a vocation), or at the very least, a meaningful, moral choice.

One of the challenges in arriving at this understanding is that many churches feel they do in fact have a meaningful ministry to singles in the church due to the presence of specialized ministry programming. For instance, singles groups increasingly appear as a distinct ministry in evangelical churches. The presence of such contexts in which singles can meet, interact, and potentially find a mate (which sometimes is even the stated purpose of such ministries) seem to demonstrate an effort to value the church's single members. However, upon closer inspection, do these customized spaces for singles yield forth a biblical understanding of singleness, or even a more developed embrace of celibacy as a calling?

An immediate concern that should be voiced with respect to some of the ministries noted above is that, by and large, these tend to focus on young singles. Here we are thinking of those 18 years and older, often thought of as young professionals. This is why the "College & Career" moniker seems so plausible as it includes both younger, college-aged persons, as well as those in the earlier stages of a working career. In some contexts, College & Career ministry and singles ministry are seen as interchangeable. However, what would the implications of such a construal be for elderly widows? Is this space in the church's life presented as a meaningful one in which they as a single person may belong? What about divorced mothers raising children, perhaps largely on their own? An honest understanding of singleness and its various permutations must recognize that some of our singles ministries may unwittingly be only appealing to young never-married persons, often still in a stage of education, and often perceived as ones who will *eventually* marry. Thus, some of these ministries do not tend toward being spaces that recognize singleness (or celibacy) as a truly meaningful spiritual vocation.

A final consideration that grows out of our recent, cultural history is the challenge homosexuality presents to the church. The influence of the LBGT (Lesbian, Bisexual, Gay, Transgender) community is nothing short of incredible given the increase in public support for legislation that supports the legal, political, economic, and social goals of their movement. The church's challenge in this environment functions on several levels. Concerning our present discussion, the challenge is how to convey to those struggling with issues of sinful, sexual attraction to resist temptation. One of the answers typically given to persons with persistent same-same attraction is that they should trust God, remain chaste, and if need-be, embrace singleness and the ultimate course of celibacy. While this plan of action (with proper biblical nuancing) may in fact be sound counsel, we must consider the significant difficulties with this advice if the church in question has not cultivated a culture of acceptance toward single members. In other words, a focus on the family that does not actually focus on God's new family in Christ, with all its sundry members (marrieds, singles, the elderly, etc.), will find it much more difficult to minister to those who struggle with sexual sin, as well as having a credible voice in the larger culture.

In view of these pressing challenges, we must reclaim a biblically serious view of the place of single members in the family of God. If generational discipleship is an enterprise for the entire church to be invested in, it will not do for the fastest growing demographic in the church to be misunderstood or bracketed out of large aspects of the ministry simply because they do not conform to the default picture of the family. A first step in ameliorating this problem would be to consider two ways the single life helps us understand the Gospel better.

Two Gospel Horizons

The church has often been held captive by a certain picture of singleness. This picture portrays singleness as an undesirable halfway house that the church must help singles escape.

Marriage, after all, is *the* institution which bears witness to Christ's love for His church. Singleness is seen as a problem to be solved. However, this picture does not square with Scripture. Here we will consider two horizons toward which faithful singleness can point.

Gospel Testimony Through Sacrificial Service

In 1 Corinthians 7, Paul explains the practical value of singleness for the cause of Christian mission and ministry. It frees up one from the domestic responsibilities which attend marriage and family, and enables them to have a more flexible life of service. However, we should be careful to note that this was not merely a practical judgment, but a theological one. For in choosing the *practical* means of service, one is also choosing a sacrificial or cruciform approach to service. This is evident in several places throughout Paul's writings and the New Testament in general, but Paul's second letter to the Corinthians helps us to see the distinct testimony for the Gospel that comes through the sacrificial choice to remain single.

Among the goals of Paul's Corinthian ministry was the goal to foster genuine Christian unity and generosity. Specifically, his desire was to see the Corinthian believers so united with Christ, each other, and the emerging Christian church that they were willing to give sacrificially to the Lord's work. Among these good works was a collection for impoverished Christians in Jerusalem. Some commentary on this collection is found across several chapters in 2 Corinthians, most notably chapters 8 and 9. One roadblock to Paul's achievement of this goal were suspicions that abounded about him in the hearts of some of the Corinthians. While it is not completely clear what the main cause of the suspicion was, it created some credibility issues for Paul's ministry.

Despite these suspicions, Paul communicates a faithful theology of giving as being grounded in the generosity of God. He writes, "For you know the grace of our Lord Jesus Christ, that though he was rich, yet for your sake he became poor, so that you by his poverty might become rich" (2 Corinthians 8:9). He also offers practical implications of such an understanding: "Whoever sows sparingly will also reap sparingly, and whoever sows bountifully will also reap bountifully" (9:6), and "God loves a cheerful giver" (7b). We should additionally observe that Paul's admonitions had greater potential of being received and embraced because Paul's lifestyle enabled him to choose to minister for free, not taking a salary for his ministry to them (1 Corinthians 9:14-15; 2 Corinthians 11:7). Despite being confronted with credibility questions, Paul was able to communicate the call to give because he had surrendered his rights to take compensation and instead worked (though he was often supported by other churches). It is no small observation that Paul's lack of familial commitments offered this flexibility, which in turn enabled him not to allow the Corinthians' giving to be hampered because they were being summoned to give by a person distrusted by some of them. His decision to forgo compensation is especially significant when considered against the backdrop of the super-apostles' influence on the Corinthians as professional teachers (see chapter 11).

This example helps one to see that the practical decision to remain single and faithfully serve while single is bound up to a conviction about the Gospel. To make such decisions for the cause of Christ reflects to the world that there is something greater worthy of one's spiritual allegiance. Choosing to utilize one's social and financial flexibility in service to the King instead of self is a powerful testimony to the infinite worth of knowing Christ. In this, a sacrificial, single lifestyle may point unbelievers to the Savior who sacrificed all for the world.

As parents and especially grandparents of the Baby Boomer Generation lament the consumer-mindset of the rising generation (fairly or unfairly), one of the many antidotes is to surround these young people with godly examples of people who have remained flexible and free for the sake of Christ's kingdom, not consumer desires. Mature singles provide such an example.

Hope for the Coming Kingdom

The transition from the Old Covenant to New represents a profound eschatological reality, which is the inauguration of Christ's Kingdom. This transition did in fact have a bearing on how marriage and procreation were configured in the biblical message. Family was not so much redefined as it was thickened due to Christ's advent. The church, which Christ instituted, would be comprised of people from every tribe, tongue, and nation. It would not be limited by ethnic ties, nor would biological relations be determinative for its membership.

In this understanding, spiritual heirs had primacy, not biological ones. Following Christ then as a single person means that one has placed their hope in something higher than the satisfaction of a happy marriage, well-adjusted children, or witnessing the birth of grandchildren.

As blessed as these things are, the hopes of the single person are to be set fully on Christ and bringing hope to others through that devotion. Indeed, even the true widows are those who are "left all alone, [having] set [their] hope on God and [continuing] in supplications and prayers night and day" (1 Timothy 5:5). Their eyes are fixed on the age to come in which the church's true groom returns, the One who has never nor will ever leave them widows. As Oliver O'Donovan notes, "Humanity in the presence of God will know a community in which the fidelity of love which marriage makes possible will be extended beyond the limits of marriage" (O'Donovan, 1994, p. 70). The early church was very effective in bearing forth this understanding of hope and witness. O'Donovan (1994) further explains,

> To this eschatological hope the New Testament church bore witness by fostering the social conditions which could support a vocation to the single life. It conceived of marriage and singleness as alternative vocations, each a worthy form of life, the two together comprising the whole Christian witness to the nature of affectionate community. The one declared that God had vindicated the order of creation, the other pointed to its eschatological transformation. But the coexistence of the two within the Christian church did not mean a loss of integrity to either. Each had to function as what it was, according to its own proper structure (p. 70).

Even in 1 Corinthians Paul notes that Christians with spouses must discover how they may "live as though they had none" (7:29b). Paul is not advocating neglect. However, the reality of the age to come has some bearing on the lives of those who have spouses also. Christ's return redefines how we think of time, knowing the present form of the world is passing away. Yet, single Christians have the opportunity and responsibility to live with unique urgency and patience.

Their hopes are set not on domestic goals, for they find rest in the all-sufficiency of a relationship with Christ and His people as their family. They also realize their service to Christ bears witness to His return.

Entailed in each of these Gospel horizons is an indication that even as the Gospel has borne witness through the faithful life of a single person, an opportunity for service is also enabled. For the D6 movement to speak of intergenerational discipleship in a comprehensive way, it must be grounded in a biblical view of the Gospel, but it must also show how that Gospel gives rise to a particular way of life. Whatever way of life we find ourselves in, in that is a particular opportunity to serve Christ's church and all the households which comprise it. This would include the opportunity to serve a neglected class of singles: widows.

Responsibility to Serve (1 Timothy 5)

We observed earlier that singleness need not only be understood as the practice of lifelong celibacy as enabled by divine gifting or calling. Singleness is a station of life that may or may not be permanent, and yet will always be (and increasingly) present in the church.

Additionally, if the Census Bureau's calculations are accurate, singleness will gradually characterize the larger society in which the church ministers. Therefore, we must not only develop a proper understanding of celibacy as a rare, but also real gift. We must also understand singleness as a station of life and the responsibilities of service that accompany it.

We know from passages like Acts 6 that the early church had some form of strategic service to widows. This knowledge comes to us by way of conflict which arises, ultimately resulting in a clarification and reorganization of administrative responsibilities among leaders in the early church. The office of deacon (or servant) is instituted to attend to the physical needs of the widows in the church, enabling the apostles (and eventually future elders) to focus on their responsibilities to preach and pray. Such a ministry was deemed so significant that Paul spends a lengthy portion of 1 Timothy 5 giving specific instructions about the church's ministry to widows—another class of singles in the ancient and contemporary church. While space does not permit an exploration of every detail of these instructions, we should observe a few features of this passage.

First, an important consideration of service includes the enlistment of children and grandchildren in helping their widowed mother or grandmother. They must "learn to show godliness to their own household and to make some return to their parents, for this is pleasing in the sight of God" (v. 4). This admonition is so significant that it is later followed by the judgment that they are "worse than an unbeliever" if they do not provide for their relatives (v. 8). Here we observe that the nuclear family as a force for social stability and provision is taken quite seriously. So while we know that the church is to be understood as the family of God, this important metaphor does not eclipse the social and economic utility of stable, loving families in society at large.

Second, widows must be properly identified in order to be enrolled for special help and regular support by the church. Verses 9-16 reiterate the need for relatives to be allowed to fulfill their responsibilities, but these verses also devote detailed attention to specific requirements of authentic widows. Here we see that the church was expected to be guided by practical considerations if they were to give help in a spiritually appropriate way. Among those potentially disqualifying factors would be if they did not have a reputation for good works and service (some examples are provided in v. 10), and if they had not been able to faithfully control their passions. Younger widows were not to be enrolled as they would inevitably choose to marry out of unbridled desire, or because they simply should remarry and establish households given the spiritual goods that would attain through such a choice.

These qualifications along with the presence of widow care itself yield several conclusions. First, the church was expected to recognize that some states of singleness (in this case that of being a widow) often created a legitimate need for the church with which to be concerned. Second, while the nuclear family unit had an immediate spiritual responsibility to address the need, the church had a responsibility to exercise prudential involvement about these situations to ensure the need was met, regardless of the party who would eventually do so. Third, the church's ministry to widows was not to function as a modern social program with no checks and balances. The moral conduct of the person in question (including prior faithfulness) shaped the church's response from situation-to-situation. Finally, the church was commanded to provide spiritual counsel and direction about even matters of marriage and remarriage. Presumably, faithful widows (or widowers) in the church were expected to heed such counsel as well.

One reason that many churches find it difficult to develop faithful ministries to singles is the unreliability of such persons. This is especially thought to be the case among younger singles. And, in fact, many young singles are perhaps spiritually immature and this leads them to postpone thinking of marital commitment. Single Christians of many ages—like singles in general—often have more disposable income to travel frequently, and thus they are often unreliable for helping in weekly ministries. However, even if we assume that *all* singles are this way, this simply heightens the need for the church to teach and model a biblical view of singleness. The specific instructions about those who constitute true widows help us to see that ministering to single members does not require a blanket endorsement of *any* expression of singleness. Some view singleness as an opportunity for furthering their own individual pursuits.

Other singles truly desire marriage and simply have been unable to attain this goal. In other words, the aforementioned New Testament passages illustrate the connection between singleness, opportunities for service, and the responsibilities to serve, which the church must take seriously. Discipleship is a free choice that flows from an authentic embrace of the Gospel, and yet it is also a sacrificial choice of one committed to service.

Strategic Opportunities for the Church

In a 2011 New York Times article, Erik Eckholm tells of an experienced, single pastor unable to find work after a lengthy search. According to Eckholm's research, most evangelical churches will never seriously consider a single pastor for fear that (a) he won't relate well to married couples, or because (b) his sexual orientation is in question (E. Eckholm, 2011).

Whatever the reason for this bias against single pastors, it is indicative of a larger failure of the evangelical church to develop a robust theology of singleness. Whether it is seeing celibacy as an ahistorical spiritual oddity never to be repeated, or singleness as a merely transitional stage, the biblical account bears witness to a more positive vision for Christian singleness. Such a vision would help the church see some of its strategic opportunities to have a thriving witness to singleness in its congregation. Here we will close with three practical areas for churches to consider in fostering a healthy congregational life for singles who will in turn help create a climate of intergenerational discipleship.

Temptation

In his excellent book on the body, Matthew Lee Anderson expresses concerns about societal myths that the church has been complicit in perpetuating. Among these myths is the one which says sexuality and wholeness are connected. In our desire to give a theological account of sexuality and gender, we convey not only that these are part of our human design, but we also suggest that to be fully human is to be engaged sexually (through matrimony of course).

However, the logic of such an understanding is that single persons by definition are incomplete. Anderson argues that this is not only unwise, but especially dangerous for younger singles. He (Anderson, 2011, p. 132) explains, "We implicitly convey to young people that sex is a need by marginalizing those who are single or cordoning them off in singles groups so that they hopefully will get married. Then we expect them to live some of the most sexually charged years of their lives without yielding to temptation. No wonder young people struggle to stay sexually pure: either sex is essential to their flourishing as humans or it isn't."

In other words, not only does such an approach fail to appreciate singleness for what it can be, but there is an added layer to the temptations that war against the souls of younger members. Anderson (2011, p. 133) further asserts that "a church without singles has lost one of its main ways of warning against a sexual idolatry that has driven the whole world mad."

Congregations need to seek to create healthy cultures of singleness in order to press back against the temptations of members to satisfy sexual desire while also remaining single. It would be a misreading to take Paul's "better to marry than to burn" admonition and press it too far in its practical thrust. To suggest that just because one struggles with sexual temptation he should automatically marry and marry soon would be tantamount to saying that because God loves a cheerful giver, we should only give when we feel cheerful. Discipleship entails the capacity to flee temptation, or to resist it whenever it rears its ugly head. Healthy single members help contribute to such a culture of discipleship in the church.

Preaching

Preaching had the capacity to build up the church as it grounds it more deeply in the grace of the Lord Jesus Christ. The hallmark of effective preaching is the bridging of the two worlds, an idea popularized by the late Anglican preacher John R. W. Stott. Some of the tools for bridging the biblical and contemporary worlds are meaningful illustrations. These come in many forms—real-life stories, personal experiences, literary references, and more. Preachers tend to work with illustrations which are more in line with the type of congregation they are preaching to, and understandably so. We also must preach *toward* the type of congregation we seek.

Illustrations can be a delimiting feature in preaching. People can come to feel the illustrations used never seem to apply to their unique situation. To be sure, it is not the responsibility of the preacher to apply every point of every message to every type of life-situation his people inhabit. Yet one wonders if the tendency of many to focus specific illustrations only on marriage or childrearing is reasonable given the number of young singles, divorcees, and widows/widowers who will sit in our pews. If preachers choose to make specific, realistic applications to everyday life a valuable aspect of their preaching, they will need to determine how to be inclusive of the variety of legitimate domestic situations represented by their people. Such preaching has the ability to affirm the unique spiritual dilemmas of their people at all stages of life, or unintentionally communicate that married persons raising children are the only ones living the faith in the world.

Image

Church historian Lauren Winner notes that "it can be dispiriting to sit alone in a church seemingly full of married couples, and many single people—generally happy, well-adjusted folks—feel utterly uncomfortable in church" (Winner, 2005, p. 136) Winner here expresses a feeling that cannot be totally ameliorated by church leaders. However, how the church shapes, structures, and presents its ministry can contribute to this discomfort or soften it. In light of all churches do to make seekers comfortable, the lack of affirmation for those living as singles is strange. The idyllic picture of the smiling couple with their arms draped over their two children (usually a boy and girl) appears on church websites, promotional literature, and increasingly in sticker form on the rear windshield of SUVS. To value singleness does not mean to cheapen or degrade marriage. But what it may require is to recognize that God has used and continues to use people from many different walks of life to embody His presence, power, and purposes.

Consider Moses who was unmarried until age 40. Abraham and Sarah were childless into their nineties. Ruth initially chose singleness in order to serve her mother-in-law. Elijah and Elisha both were single. And Jeremiah was called to singleness and preached for 50 years to a non-repentant people. These men and women of God likely would not thrive in today's church, nor appear on the cover of the new church pictorial directory. Yet in our fallen world a Gospel-centered church can consist of singles, widows, and divorcees, in addition to couples. The church then must be presented as a place for the nations, for prayer, for sinners, and for singles.

Conclusion

Jesus taught that there would be no marriage in the life to come (Matthew 22:23-28). Such a realization does not cheapen marriage in the present life; rather, it informs how it may obtain its greater good for the sake of Christ, even in a fallen world. In the meantime, the church must learn how it can embrace and encourage those who have been given the gift of celibacy to embrace it faithfully. Singleness is a matter of discipleship as it has the potential to faithfully bear witness to the Gospel. Of the church, Dietrich Bonhoeffer once said, "the world becomes too confining; all its hopes and dreams are set on the Lord's return" (Bonhoeffer, 2003, p. 250).

Singles must be taught to model this hope, and in so doing they will increasingly help strengthen the link between church and home.

References

Anderson, M. L. (2011). *Earthen vessels: Why our bodies matter to our faith*. Bloomington, MN: Bethany House.

Bonhoeffer, D. (2003). *Discipleship*. Minneapolis, MN: Fortress Press.

Camosy, C. (2013). *For love of animals: Christian ethics, consistent action.* New York, NY: Franciscan Media.

Eckholm, E. (2011). "Single and Evangelical? Good Luck Finding Work as a Pastor." Retrieved on 12 May, 2011 from http://www.nytimes.com/2011/03/22/us/22pastor.html?_r=3&partner=rss&emc=rss.

Köstenberger, A. & Jones, D. (2010). *God, marriage, and family: Rebuilding the biblical foundations.* Wheaton, IL: Crossway.

O'Donovan, O. (1994). *Resurrection and moral order: An outline of evangelical ethics.* Grand Rapids, MI: Eerdmans.

Unmarried and Single Americans Week Sept. 16-22, 2012. Retrieved on 17 October 2015 from https://www.census.gov/newsroom/releases/archives/facts_for_features_special_editions/cb12-ff18.html.

Watts, W. J. (2015). "Singleness as Discipleship." 2015 Free Will Baptist Symposium Digest of Papers. Randall University, Moore, Oklahoma.

Winner, L. (2005). *Real sex: The naked truth about chastity.* Grand Rapids, MI: Brazos Press.

Author Biography

W. Jackson Watts is the pastor of Grace Free Will Baptist Church in the greater St. Louis area, where he has served since 2011. Jackson is a founding member of the The Helwys Society Forum.

Practitioner Insights

The D6 Family Journal editorial board helped design the uniqueness of this journal. This section entitled Practitioner Insights offers you a look at family ministry from practitioners engaged in preschool, children, student, college, adults, or senior ministry. The practitioner reflections do not submit to the same academic peer review process but still pass through multiple editors before becoming part of the volume. We believe this section will allow insightful ministry leaders the chance to present an area facing the church today.

Counseling Christian Teens Struggling With Same-Sex Attraction

Dr. Ken Coley

Paul was never in a rush to leave his 7th period Bible class, but Mrs. James noticed that today he lingered longer than usual. Mrs. James glanced up from her laptop to see him shifting from foot to foot, trying to speak but choking on every syllable. Identifying that this young man was agonizing over an important issue, she closed her computer and invited her student to have a seat as she pulled her chair around to face him. Glancing over the student's shoulder, she took note that her classroom door was open, but no one was nearby in the hall. As she settled into her chair, she assumed a relaxed posture, not wanting to communicate to the seventeen-year-old that she was alarmed. After a few moments, Paul began, "As we read Romans today in class, I felt really guilty because I think that I am gay…"

The presence of the topic of homosexuality in every medium of our students' lives demands that we prepare ourselves as educators to assist them in confronting this issue. Everywhere a member of our society turns, he or she hears another spokesperson endorsing life styles that are diametrically opposed to biblical instruction. But we should not be dismayed—this challenge to God's standards has been with mankind since the earliest generations.

Are teenagers growing up in Christian environments immune from these temptations? We would be naïve to think we can put a protective cocoon around them. So, in light of this, *to what extent are our classroom teachers prepared to assist students like Paul in the scenario above?*

With these concerns in mind the author of this article asked a series of eight questions to four experienced Christian counselors. The four contributors were recruited from four different regions of the United States. Each has training in counseling teenagers and three of the four have at least ten years or more of serving in a Christian school. Their responses were compiled, and the researcher coded them for consistent themes. A draft article was assembled and returned to the expert panel for changes and clarification. This article was approved by each respondent. The participants thought it best to go by the initials of the states in which each lives. [PA resides in Pennsylvania, KY in Kentucky, TX in Texas, and ID in Idaho.] Here are some of their insights accompanied by the researcher's summary of their coaching:

Is this a realistic situation? (A student approaches a Christian school teacher about feelings or thoughts about being gay.)

The thoughtful answers of the four counselors all touched on a key concept—establishing trusting relationships. In an environment where such relationships exist, there is a possibility that this conversation will take place. Absent a trusting relationship, our participants believe that it is very unlikely.

KY: As they get older, students develop stronger relationships and may ask a teacher, if they feel love and support. Developing relationships with students is vital to our role as Christian educators. Hopefully the school environment encourages meaningful relationships.

PA: It is possible, but not too likely. It will depend upon the relationship the student has with the teacher. For the teacher, tuning in to his or her sense of seriousness will have everything to do with the rest of an approach to her or him.

PA: Key for any confidant is to be able to "hear" what the student's concern(s) is (are).

ID: While it is not very realistic that a student in a Christian school would announce that he is gay because students know they couldn't stay in the school at that point, it is realistic that a student would start a conversation about the subject with a trusted teacher to figure out what is going on with their own feelings and urges. This would come from an anxious or tormented kid that needed some answers.

TX: Yes, absolutely! Christian educators tell me questions *they* are being asked by their students…and this is one. Whether a teacher would be approached has to do with the *approachability of the teacher* and *the relationship with the student*, as well as the teacher's reputation.

Christian educators in my network experience an increasing acceptance from parents asserting being gay is morally neutral. Thus, this relatively new worldview not only will influence children, but also will open the door to experimentation.

What Scripture should a teacher share with a student who expresses these concerns? (No need for a lengthy doctrinal discussion...the focus is to equip teachers)

Three respondents stated at the beginning of their reactions to this question: listening at this point is more important than presenting Scripture. The teacher must build trust and reinforce the student's confidence that his teacher cares about the pain he is experiencing. Communicate understanding and compassion in your verbal and non-verbal responses.

KY: If Scripture is used in the first response, it will shut a student down. A simple Bible answer will communicate a lack of understanding of the depth of their pain in this incredibly difficult struggle. After you have established unconditional love, asking them where God fits into their struggle would be helpful in understanding if that matters to them, and how you can proceed.

PA: I'm not sure Scripture should be used at the outset with such a student. The point is to listen and build deeper trust, but also to understand what thoughts are giving him/her this worry that he/she is gay.

PA: Scripture that is always relevant is that which confirms the love of Christ to sinners—"When I want to do good, evil is present with me" Romans 7:21. No believer is without that conflict in one way or another. And Romans 8:1 follows: "There is no condemnation to those in Christ."

ID: There needs to be a great deal of listening and understanding before God's truth is shared. Kids have varying ability to take in truth depending on their emotional state and current openness, so teachers need to be very discerning as they share the Word.

Gently talking about how God has created us to live in sexual purity and how the world has perverted that is important.

TX: Explain how strugglers can establish their identity in Christ. "It is for freedom that Christ has set us free. Stand firm, then, and do not let yourselves be burdened again by a yoke of slavery" (Galatians 5:1, NIV). Teach students their true identity in Christ through memorization and meditation: "Do you not know that your bodies are temples of the Holy Spirit, who is in you, whom you have received from God? You are not your own" (1 Corinthians 6:19, NIV).

What counseling approaches or models might help a teacher in this situation? (Based on your training, both biblical and secular, is there a model of counseling that would help here?)

Though some of the coaching suggestions that follow may intersect with existing models of counseling, three of our counselors discouraged viewing this situation through the lens of one particular approach or paradigm.

KY: Bond with them, struggle with them, LOVE them unconditionally. First they need to know they are loved. Spending a good amount of time with the student and demonstrating that they are loved is vital.

PA: Listening to the student, loving the student, and finding out the severity of the students' concern are paramount. The teacher needs to know that, from God's perspective, homosexuality is a choice—it doesn't happen to you and is not "caused" by something in you. Each of us have features about us, because of heredity and environment, that may make it easier to lean in one sinful direction or another and that may make our battle with certain sins more acute. The aphorism of Luther fits here—"you can't keep the birds from flying over your head, but you can keep them from building a nest in your hair."

ID: The teacher needs to really listen—to words, to body language, to underlying feelings. A listening response is leaning toward the student, being open in body language and attitude. The teacher needs to clarify occasionally, ask questions, and summarize periodically just to make sure he understands. The teacher just needs to hang in there with the kid because this kind of situation can be emotionally draining and intimidating for someone not used to it. I also usually ask students where they are with God. By this time, kids are really honest in their answers and what I share from God's Word depends on whether they know God, are seeking Him, or are closed off. I often conclude a session with both giving of hope and an action step. The action is extremely variable. It could be meeting again, making a step by step plan, reading verses, referral to outside counselor, or a vast number of other possibilities.

TX: A counseling model known as Reparative Therapy (or sexual-orientation conversion therapy) has helped many strugglers change their sexual orientation from homosexual to heterosexual. God would never call anyone to change without giving that person the ability to change. 1 Thessalonians 5:24 says, "The one who calls you is faithful, and he will do it." I have seen God deliver countless strugglers from a deeply ingrained homosexual lifestyle. Christian educators need to help struggling students to determine: If they have an authentic relationship with Christ and if they don't, then I encourage the teacher to help lead the students to surrender their lives to Christ.

What advice do you have for an administrator to fashion a policy regarding a teacher placed in this situation?

With some qualifications, three respondents believe there is no need for a specific policy. The one who believes there is a need for such a policy emphasized the need for privacy and confidentiality. There was a clear distinction in the minds of the participants between students struggling with "feelings" as opposed to "actions that violate existing policies." The insights below clarify this distinction:

KY: It is important that teachers use the school counselor as a resource. I don't know that the teacher should be required to tell the administration, unless the student has acted on their feelings. We should not have a policy on feelings. Most of these students haven't acted out yet, and need to be able to process. I believe there are usually other issues surrounding same sex attraction, and a professional counselor can help.

PA: No sin is beyond the reach of God's grace except the "unpardonable" one. And this is not it. It is serious, destructive, etc. but it is forgivable and changeable, by God's grace. The policy should allow the teacher to meet with such a student and to detect the seriousness of it with him or her. As with any area of sin, if there is seriousness on the part of the student about the thought level and feeling level and if there is movement toward change and accountability with the teacher or school counselor, by God's grace, this can rest with the student and teacher/counselor.

The teacher should work toward urging the student (in most situations) to share this battle and any steps of help with his or her parents. But that should probably NOT be the first thing the teacher decides to do or talk about with the teen. Equally important would be the offer to be with the student when he does talk to his parents—for support and clarification of the issues to the parents about the student's maturity for coming for help.

ID: I see no need for a policy. If the school has hired mature, godly teachers who love students and have a fresh, daily walk with God, they will respond to students in the right way.

TX: Policies should protect the student's privacy and confidentiality. Some schools have a policy that a teacher must *never promise* confidentiality to a student regarding a private conversation. Teachers should consider reporting to an administrator if he or she believes the information may result in harm to the student or to others. Sexual activity can fall under this category.

Should the expression of guilt or concern result in a conference with parents or a notification to other school leaders?

Partnership with parents is one of the hallmarks of the Christian school movement, so it naturally follows that teachers would be concerned about sharing this scenario with the student's parents. How did our panel respond? "Not necessarily." They encourage the teacher involved to gauge the level of severity or distress and the degree of actual involvement. Check out their discussion below:

KY: Each family situation can be so different. However, allowing the student to keep what they have told confidential is important. Teachers don't have the same advantage. I would refer them to professional counseling and keep it confidential from the administration. The student needs to know that confidentiality is kept unless by law, then the counselor is required to inform.

PA: If he has acted out or these are life-dominating things, then, yes, a conference with the parents is warranted. It is no longer just a private battle in his mind and soul. The goal of the teacher should be to get the teen to be willing to attend the conference and express his thoughts about what is going on—especially if there is a repentant spirit and concern for the right reasons.

ID: Not necessarily. If the student just needs processing, support, and information, it would not result in a conference or notification. However, if the student seemed really distressed and needed outside counseling or a visit to his pastor, I would definitely involve the parents. The younger the child and the more serious the situation, the more likely parent involvement would be.

TX: The best-practice among Christian educators is to treat situations involving homosexuality like any issue involving sexual immorality.
- Address the *heart issue* first—discerning the heart and intent of the student.
- Approach the student with counsel rather than discipline while requiring parents to become involved in the counseling process.
- In the case of an uncooperative or unrepentant student, handle this situation as a disciplinary issue and involve the parents as well.
- Notify the school administration.

Do middle school students and high school students differ in their expression of gay/lesbian concerns?

Every experienced teacher is familiar with the precociousness of some middle schoolers, but at the same time understand the developmental differences between middle and high school students. Here's what the experienced counselors think:

KY: Middle schoolers have not usually acted on their feelings and it would be very important that they receive counseling. Parents would have to be involved to receive the help they need. Carefully helping a student understand that counseling will help them deal with this is very important.

PA: My work with high school students would lead me to think they will have thought about these matters regarding themselves, their parents, and their friends more seriously than a middle-schooler. High school students may develop rigorous rationalizations and have more of a sense of the effects from homosexual thoughts.

ID: I think middle school girls experiment with "risky" lesbian behavior more than older girls. I also think the boys—middle school through 9th grade might be more inclined to experiment.

TX: Middle-schoolers generally don't have access to transportation and consequently their sexual activities tend to be more virtual, experimenting with virtual chatting/flirting and interaction with strangers.

Are you familiar with any legal issues that come into play in this situation?

PA: Obviously the confidentially matter enters the picture here. Privileged information (different from confidentially) is a foggy area too. Both would, it seems to me, make it imperative for the teacher to work with the student to talk to his parents about this—at some point.

ID: Bullying and harassment is a legal issue and a school rule issue. We would have the legal right to expel a student for being openly gay even though it is not stated explicitly in the handbook.

TX: A lawsuit in my state involved the expulsion of a student for an incident involving homosexuality. The court upheld the school's position.

Do you have any other areas of concern?

The research concluded with an open-ended question that allowed our experts to return the discussion to the topic of demonstrating Christ-like compassion to a fellow believer who is struggling to honor the Lord.

KY: I am concerned that we as Christian educators may not understand the depth of pain these students are in. Allowing a student time to work through the issue is important to their future and how they continue in their spiritual walk.

PA: Another area of concern, in general, is that the sin of homosexuality becomes more significant than other sins and looks like it is out of reach of the grace of God for forgiveness and change.

ID: The main tact I have taken with students who talk with me about homosexual worries or experiences is to normalize it as a limited event or passing thought that many kids have.

I have found this to be an immense relief to students. Homosexuality is so normalized in our culture that kids are curious and do some experimenting. This is wrong, but it does not make them homosexual.

TX: *Never* condone or participate in gay "bashing." We are to love the sinner and hate the sin.

Conclusion

Throughout the Gospels we see snapshots in every chapter of Christ patiently assisting His contemporaries sort out their dilemmas...Theological struggles that seem to have them at an impasse. How do we show compassion without communicating that sin can be winked at? Should we express condemnation or tolerance or nothing? He always took care to link grace and faith and the importance of change.

Whether you are a parent, a Bible study leader for a group of teens, or a professional educator, it is important to take away from the responses of the four experienced counselors who were interviewed for this research article the significance of establishing trusting relationships and the importance of providing a compassionate, non-threatening ear. This generation is surrounded by siren calls like no generation before them and will be tempted beyond imagination. We must be prepared to stand firm in biblical teaching while bearing their burdens with them.

Author Biography

Ken Coley is the Senior Professor of Christian Education and Director of Ed.D. Studies at Southeastern Baptist Theological Seminary.

A Practical Strategy for Partnering With the Family
Phil Bell

I recently completed my first half-marathon! If you've ever completed a long distance run, you know the combination of pain and exhilaration at the finish line is incredible! For me, the last three miles were quite challenging, but fortunately a newfound friend called Ray helped me get across the finish line. At two miles to go, Ray asked me a pertinent question: "What's your purpose for running this half-marathon?" In the next half a mile, gasping for air, I shared that I was driven by a vision to get healthy, stay active with my kids, and hopefully live longer than my late father (who passed away in his early fifties). Being reminded of that vision and being urged along by Ray helped me finish strong.

Having a vision to live longer, while leaving a lasting legacy with my own family is what drives me to get up early and force myself to run long distances. (It's also become my best thinking time.) However, since the race, I have come to the realization that vision alone was not enough. Rather, it was a compelling vision *combined* with a strategic training plan that helped me run the race effectively.

Now make the leap with me as I jump from marathons to ministry. Go back to Ray's question and consider your ministry: What's your purpose? It's likely you can go back to a significant moment in time that compelled you to begin your ministry journey. Go back to the start line right now and rediscover that moment… What makes you get up in the morning these days? What's *your* vision?

As you consider these important questions that will help you over the finish line, don't lose focus on the steps needed to get you there. You see, vision alone is not enough. It is a compelling vision combined with a strategic plan that will help you and I effectively reach and equip the next generation for Christ.

The challenge many of us face is not a lack of vision, rather a lack of strategy. Most ministry leaders I meet can provide me with a compelling vision and many can even describe their family ministry philosophy. In fact, that used to be me until the team of people I led kept asking: "But what does that really look like?" Or, "What's the specific strategy to implement this vision and philosophy?" And here's what I found: If I can't determine the strategy, my team will tend to default back to what they have always done. In other words, we find ourselves running back to a church centric model that focuses exclusively on the weekend or midweek programs, while missing our opportunities to connect church with home. In addition, it's imperative that we establish a simple, reproducible, and strategic plan that any staff member or volunteer can implement. If a strategy is riddled with complexity, it will likely never see longevity.

What follows is a strategic template for our family ministry, along with defining statements that are helping us move beyond a church centric model to a family equipping model. Churches need a family ministry strategy where the principles can be adopted, adapted, and implemented at every level of the organization, and by anyone.

ENVIRONMENTS: *We provide safe, relevant, and fun environments centered around biblical truth, where children, students, parents/guardians can take next steps in their faith journey.*

You've created the weekend and midweek environments. You've worked hard to make them safe, relevant, fun, and built around biblical truth. But what happens when your children and students leave? What have you done in your environments to set up the next step?

Do our current environments focus on spoon feeding content, rather than stirring up relevant questions to create ongoing conversations? Do our families show up to consume rather than being compelled to apply what they have been learning? What crucial questions are we sending kids home to grapple with? What essential action steps are we giving our families when they leave us?

In our context, we're not content to provide a great weekend experience for our kids without a compelling next step for them and their parents/guardians. As an example, our goal is to have every small group leader provide a specific challenge or next step for our kids to take home. This is also communicated to parents/guardians through a number of different modes. We'll talk about that next…

ENGAGE: *We communicate consistently and relevantly in multiple modes in order to reach and engage the children, students, and parents/guardians.*

You and I have the lifesaving Gospel to share. You and I could well have the most impactful environments for the family to hear the Gospel. However, without effective engagement the message is lost.

Communicate. Families today communicate in numerous modes, so should we! While one parent will prefer to read an email, another will take a print copy to hang on the fridge. (We are that family. Our fridge is full of reminders and artwork our kids have created). While some are connected to social media, others are dependent on a reminder text message from us.

Promotion Dilution. The challenge we face however is that families today live in a world of promotion dilution where they receive literally thousands of messages to engage in numerous places throughout their week. Our communication can quickly become diluted in a sea of competing messages. This explains why so many parents will often claim to have not seen our communications. It's possible our message has been lost in a world of competing messages. Do we think that an announcement on a piece of paper and a reminder email will be enough?

In a world of competing messages, it's imperative to employ strategic, simple, and consistent modes of communication. Effective engagement requires us to communicate in numerous modes and multiples times during any given week. But where will we find the time to keep communicating effectively? In our context, we have come to rely on scheduling systems and apps that allow us to schedule our email, social media, and text reminders. It takes some work ahead of time, but once the system is in place, it works its magic in the background while we work elsewhere. It goes without saying that a website that is continuously updated (and promoted) goes a long way.

Listen. While effective communication is a good start, it can never be a replacement for relationships with parents. In other words, good communication allows us to knock on the door of parents, while relationships earn us an invite into their home. For us, we have found that holding focus groups with parents has allowed us to sit and listen to parents of various aged children and students. Our time together is relaxed and focused on listening to them by using two or three questions to glean insights to their world. Ask some simple yet strategic questions: "When we say that we are here to partner with parents, what does that mean to you? What can we do to partner with you to help you succeed in greater ways at home?" These questions have produced a gold mine of insights, ideas, and improvements to all that we do. It's not rocket science, but it's a lost art these days. Just listen.

ENCOURAGE: *We assist parents/guardians in connecting intentionally with other parents/guardians who are on the same faith journey.*

Parents need to know they are not alone in their journey and need to be encouraged by others who understand their situations. In a picture perfect world where we are constantly posting the best parts of our family, it can be easy to feel a failure. Parents need to be in community with those who are on a similar journey along with those parents who are a few steps ahead of them.

Connect Intentionally. We are striving to find opportunities for parents to connect intentionally, through our classes and events, while also being huge promoters of our small group ministry. The key, however, is not to create more events on an already packed calendar. Rather, it's creating opportunities within the environments we already have in place.

What could this look like? It's the end of summer camp for your student ministry. The students are arriving back at 2:00 p.m. on Sunday, but you have parents show up at 1:15 p.m. In 45 minutes, you can have parents get to know each other, share about their students, and then provide them with an overview of the camp along with conversation starters and next steps. Or, alternatively: You've created a class for parents to learn how to share Christ with their children. You could sit parents in rows and be focused on teaching content, or you could sit them in circles and give them some discussion questions as well as teach them content.

Parents spoke and we listened. In our discussions and surveys with parents, they told us clearly that they would rather see a class extended another week if it meant they had more connection time with other parents. Parents need to know they are not alone on their island of parenthood. We can help them begin to build bridges to community and find much needed encouragement.

One last thought. Remember Ray, my half-marathon finish line buddy? What I never told you is that this guy was two decades older than me, but this was not his first half-marathon either. I can't tell you how incredible it was to run alongside a guy who knew how to finish well and to feel the confidence from someone who had gone before me. Now, being a parent is far more challenging than running any marathon, but can you imagine the impact a group of empty nesters could have on the parents in your family ministry? How are you actively inviting and involving this experienced group into the lives of your parents who need someone to run alongside them?

EQUIP: *We provide relevant and practical coaching to equip children, students, and parents/guardians to continue to take next steps at home in their faith journey.*

To put it simply, equipping parents involves developing their understanding of their role, while also providing a framework they can use at home. In other words, we coach them with knowledge while also giving them the skills to succeed at home.

What could this look like? An example of this can be seen in Deuteronomy 6:4-9. First, we can teach parents the biblical blueprint for passing on their faith to their children. Then we provide them four specific ways to bring faith into the everyday moments: 1) At mealtimes at home, 2) Driving in the car (walking along the road), 3) At bedtime, and 4) In the morning.

What works best for your parents? Building an intentional framework where we cast vision and provide practical teaching is imperative if we want to see faith come alive at home. But knowing parents' schedules, it's essential we honor their time with relevant felt needs topics, while incorporating foundational teaching that practically equips. A formal class, parent summit, short video teaching, or podcast are all ways to equip parents.

My plate is full! It's likely that you have your plate full and do not have a great deal of margin to coach and equip parents. However, there are some great organizations out there that have already done it for you. The good folks at ParentMinistry.net have already made an incredible start in this area. What about the experts in your church and community? What parents have experience in crucial areas that other parents are dying to hear?

EMPOWER: *We provide resources, tools, and experiences to empower children, students, and parents/guardians to take next steps at home in their faith journey.*

Equipping parents has been described as providing parents knowledge while also coaching them in the skills to succeed at home. Empowering them is simply pointing them to the resources and help that they can utilize as they invest in their child's faith journey.

What could this look like? You've recently equipped parents with a biblical framework and provided them with some essential skills. You took time to talk through the four everyday moments in a child's day and now parents are excited to begin. They are looking to you for ideas and resources. In your planning, you found four different devotional books for kids, along with five websites packed full of ideas and articles. When Christmas arrives, you and a team of incredible volunteers create an advent calendar with discussion questions, family activities, and links to some amazing Christmas videos that families can watch together... Get the idea?

You don't need to be the expert! I used to think I had to be expert for parents and be the source of knowledge. Now, while many parents see you as the expert, it's impossible to be the expert of everything there is to know. However, it does not mean that you can't become an expert of resources that are available to help parents succeed at home. If you haven't already, begin to build a portfolio of your go-to websites, books, and family activities. In addition, consider the following ideas:

- Ask key parents and volunteers to help you create a definitive list of resources for parents/guardians
- Ask parents to read and review books and post their reviews on a blog, along with a list of additional books
- Provide links to websites and blogs that will help parents be better resourced at home
- Post a very short weekly summary video on your website and/or social media that covers what children/students learned along with their next step
- Provide a weekly take home sheet along with a family activity as children leave your weekend experience
- Seek out experts and resources in your community that you can provide to parents who are in need of counselors, doctors, etc.

- Create a resource center at the entrance to your children's/student area. Provide sample books, a list of essential reading and websites, along with a weekly take home sheet.

In my experience, providing great resources (especially when it meets a felt need of a parent) can be the turning point for a parent to see the church being in partnership with them. So often we want parents to know information about our events and programs. However, when we can discover and distribute great resources to empower them at home, it is more likely they will tune into the great events and programs that will become the catalyst to faith conversations at home.

Finish Well! In preparation for my half-marathon, a wise friend told me that starting slow and finishing strong go hand in hand. It's true for making an eternal impact in your ministry. While this blueprint is helping us transition to a family equipping model of ministry, it's crucial to understand that some aspects have taken a while to build while others are still in formation. For us, it's been essential to take baby steps and add to the five areas slowly. As you pray and consider how to implement this framework into your ministry, ensure that you have a long-term outlook. Start slow and finish strong.

Author Biography

Phil Bell is a Family Ministry pastor from England now living in Raleigh, NC. A nationally known speaker, Phil is also a noted columnist, author, and blogger.

The Role of Games in Discipleship
by Jon Forrest

I hate stories like this. I play out youth group tragedies in my mind all the time. I get physically ill when I hear one of my worst fears actually happened to a group like this.

I know this pastor of a small group who scheduled a family style lock-in. He chose to have his devotion time around midnight in a stuffy room with terrible air conditioning.

One of the young boys who, more than likely, had not been engaged by the group slipped to the back of the room and sat in a window they had opened to get a little airflow. It's hard to say whether he sat there for the fresh air or to see the more interesting activities going on outside.

The cool air paired with the long-winded speaker and the fact that the boy had not become involved with the service eventually got the best of him. This was way more than nodding off. This was slobber-inducing hibernation sleep.

Regrettably, in his sleep, the boy fell out the window. It would have been comical if it hadn't been a third-floor window. The boy died from a lack of engagement. And you thought that hole in the wall from your last lock-in was bad.

Fortunately, the pastor was the apostle Paul. He went down and raised Eutychus from the dead. If you can raise the dead, engaging students is not quite as important.

Maybe I'm being a little tough on Paul. Can you imagine how engaging he was? With that Road to Damascus story, I'm going to say he probably didn't need Mental Ping Pong to get kids to wake up and listen to him. But as I read Acts 20:7-11, it's apparent that even Paul had students who were difficult to incorporate into the conversation with the group.

Finding those points of engagement is absolutely vital. I'm not talking about amusement. "Amusement" is a terrible word. To "muse" is to think about something deeply. So when we add the negative prefix "a" to "muse" we are saying that we are turning people's brains off. That is exactly the opposite of what we are trying to achieve with games as a tool in discipleship. Our aim is not amusement. We are shooting for fun "musement."

Teaching Students Is Like Feeding Bears in Captivity

If people were data recorders we would not need games. Imagine the ease of being able to hit a round, red, record button in student's brains and then just filling them with information. I'm about to make up a stat here. Students only absorb every 19th word you say. You can help this a little by mixing in the words "hanky-panky," "fleek," and "Imax."

Students are suffering from information over-saturation. It reminds me of a time when I was a kid and went to Pigeon Forge on vacation with my family. The Smoky Mountains were our vacation spot. We would always drive through the countryside hoping to see a bear. Other than the occasional hay bale, my imagination turned into a bear, we never had any luck spotting them. So, you can imagine my excitement when I saw the souvenir shop that advertised "Come Feed the Live Black Bears."

I begged dad until he took me. Near this huge concrete pit, we bought a third of a loaf of bread to feed this awesome creature. I was so excited until I looked down into the pit and saw a bear who looked like if he ate one more slice of bread he might explode. The floor of this sad structure was littered with stale bread that countless ignorant kids before had tried to force-feed this guy. The disappointed kid next to me threw a slice of bread that landed on the poor creature's back. "Yogi" didn't even acknowledge it.

This is a lot like our students. Can you even begin to fathom the amount of information they are bombarded with? Even content they love is swiped upwards or sideways in less than a second. How in the world can we be sure they hear the only message that counts? That is not an exaggeration either. Compared to the gospel, everything else is rubbish.

Priming Students to Learn

Students must be primed for this message of life. My lesson in priming was incredibly frustrating. I wanted to make a duck race game. So, I bought these two cast iron water pumps like Laura Ingalls might use. It was so cool. I mounted the pumps on 55 gallon drums and ran gutters away from the pumps for 8 feet, then curved it to bring the water back toward the pump where it emptied back into the drum. When you put a rubber duck in the gutter in front of the spout and started pumping, it would race through the gutter and end up back in front of you. At least that was the plan.

I built the whole set up. I put a duck in place and started pumping the handle like a wild man. Nothing happened. I pumped harder and still nothing. I took the pump back off the barrel and as I stuffed it back into the box I noticed the instructions. The little paper said "cebar la bomba antes de su uso." When I turned it over to the English side of the instructions, it said "pump must be primed before use." I poured a little water down into the pump and began pumping the handle and out flowed a rolling river that merrily floated my little duck on his way.

Students are a lot like that. The priming process of playing a game does a few things. Students are much more likely to become engaged in the conversation if they are enjoying themselves. It relaxes them and breaks the silence barrier. You will have an easier time connecting with them if they like you. Not to mention your job becomes way easier if they like the person next to them as well.

Author Biography

Jon Forrest is the youth pastor at Bethel Church in Ashland City, TN. He is a frequently requested speaker at youth events and conferences, and serves as a member of the board of Pleasant View Christian School.

Ministering to Widows and Widowers With Children in the Home

by David Lytle

The biblical mandate is clear—"look after orphans and widows in their distress" (James 1:27, NIV). Just as orphans need more than food and shelter, the widow or widower needs more than financial assistance. Like the orphan, the greatest need for the widow or widower is the need for relationship.

I am a widower. When I lost my wife of ten years, I was left to raise three small children. My experience speaks to how beautiful God's church can be in times of hardship and grief. While my pain is not unique, I have come to learn that in many ways my experience of a supporting church is rare.

My wife's death was unexpected. She was 32 and in seemly great health. We had been on the mission field for five years when she died and the children and I were forced to move back to the States. We were welcomed back by our home church with open arms and open hearts. My family was given money, food, furniture, shelter, and we were surrounded by people who cared. At one point, I got to tell my neighbor my story. He cursed when he heard about my wife's death and then he praised God when he heard what the church had done for me. "That is what the church is supposed to be!" he exclaimed. I can't help but think of Jesus' words in the Sermon on the Mount: "Let your light shine before others, so that they may see your good works and give glory to your Father who is in heaven" (Matthew 5:16, ESV).

Unfortunately, many Christians don't get the chance to tell their neighbors and co-workers how excellent their church was during their time of loss. In preparation for this article, I talked to some friends that are widows or widowers. While my research was limited in scope, I found that those who attended larger churches (over 1,000) were not cared for as well as those that attended smaller churches. One man reported that in a church of over 20 pastors, not one of them reached out in a meaningful way. He felt that pastors are just as ill-prepared in talking to those experiencing grief as regular church members. While he is still faithful to his church, he only has pastoral support from a pastor of another church.

If your church doesn't minister to the widowed it's little more than a concert venue. Both Testaments are clear on the subject. While the New Testament church is not charged with the same prescriptions as the people of God in the Old Testament, Apostolic teaching is even more emphatic. New Testament ecclesiology even dedicates a position, the Deacon, for responsibilities such as this. Moreover, just about every American congregation has multiple members who have been widowed. While the ministry details will look different depending on the congregation, I want to offer a list from my experience of the most fundamental needs churches can meet for widows and widowers.

1. Financial needs are often the most urgent and obvious from the outside looking in. The people of God generally do well in this area. As previously mentioned, my story highlights the significance of sacrificial financial stewardship in this area. Not only are we obeying the teaching of Christ and His apostles by giving to those in need, we are witnessing to our larger community. For people like my neighbor who are jaded by their negative experiences with the church, it can be a powerful apologetic.

2. Not all widows or widowers need financial assistance, but all need practical help in one way or another. For me it was the lawn. Thanks to my church family, I moved into a house with a yard for my children to play in, but I didn't know how I was going to mow the grass with no one at home to look after the one-year-old. Without me saying a word, a deacon in our church called me up and told me that he was going to bring one of the teens over to mow my grass each week. They didn't charge me, but I did volunteer to donate money to the teen mission trip. Thanks to a proactive church leader, it was a thing of beauty. It was member care. It was youth ministry. It was missions. It was everything the church should be, but so rarely is. And it all started when a leader took initiative.

3. Many widows and widowers need help with their children. While most people who are widowed have grown children, there are still many, like myself, who have the responsibility of single parenting thrust upon them. It's impossible to put into words how difficult it is to simultaneously grieve and raise children alone. In many ways, this is the situation for all single parents, not just the widowed. They are all grieving the loss of a

relationship while taking care of their children. Single parents desperately need the help of the church. Grocery shopping and babysitting are two very simple and practical ways to help a single parent in need. Sometimes they need babysitting just so they can go grocery shopping! One time a friend caught me leaving a grocery store with the three kids after a long day of work. He later told me that he felt helpless as he watched me leaving the store. He had never realized how something as simple as getting some milk could be so difficult when having to take three young kids into the store. Single-parenting is hard. Like all difficult situations, it can be the church's time to shine.

4. Widows and widowers need help managing grief. Pastors must equip their grieving members with a solid theology of Christian hope that is rooted in the resurrection of the Son of God rather than the well-meaning, but empty, platitudes that seem to be the standard in many churches. Grieving people generally deplore counterfeit optimism. They need the God that weeps beside them while still proclaiming that He is the "resurrection and the life" (John 11:25). Aside from astute theological guidance, our Pastors must be knowledgeable of the psychology of the grieving process in order to minister adequately to the grieving. Church buildings and homes can and should serve as a venue for both informal and formal grief counseling. Providing opportunities for widows and widowers to build networks dedicated to sharing their pain and struggle, is an invaluable service that is best facilitated by the local church. Often times these ministries can be led by someone who has experienced deep loss and would love an opportunity to help others.

5. Most importantly, widows and widowers need relationship. Like all good ministry, this ministry requires a committed personal relationship. This need is especially acute for widows and widowers, because this is exactly what has been stolen from them. My friend's experience of being ignored by church members and leaders is remarkably common. This is probably because most people are paralyzed by the fear of saying something hurtful. Rather than providing authentic companionship, most church members only offer pity. Pity is useless, but conversation is life-giving. Churches can counteract this paralysis by training their members to minister to widows and widowers. The most important lesson to be learned in this training is that church members must be proactive in developing re-

lationship with widows and widowers. With very few exceptions, everyone who has lost a spouse is crushingly lonely. An invitation to dinner or coffee, if accompanied by a conversation, could save a life. It saved mine.

Author Biography

David Lytle is a history teacher and former missionary to Indonesia and Peru who now resides in California.

Book Reviews

The book reviews submitted offer a critique of some of the latest family ministry titles. If you would like to see a title reviewed in the future, please submit at least two copies of either the book or galley copy (Publisher's PDF proof is acceptable if not yet published or to galley stage).

Thom S. Rainer and Jess W. Rainer, *The Millennials: Connecting to America's Largest Generation.* Nashville, TN: B&H, 2011. 304 pages. $22.99. Hardcover.

Review by Christopher Talbot, Teacher at Welch College in Gallatin, TN. Chris teaches courses in Youth and Family Ministry and Biblical studies, while also serving as the Pastor of Youth and Family at Sylvan Park Free Will Baptist Church.

The "Bridger" Generation, Generation Tech, Boomer Babies, Echo Boom, Generation Next, Generation Y, Generation XX, (10) and so on—the proposed labels are as diverse as the assorted group of people they seek to define. Nevertheless, the term "Millennial" has seemed to stick for the children of the Baby Boomer generation. Churches, denominations, and businesses alike have sought to better understand this new and complex social generation. A quick online query will reap a myriad of blog posts explaining how one might better "reach" this group. Yet, no matter how many bullet-point lists prescribed, the millennial generation still seems nebulous in their characteristics.

In seeking to do generational discipleship as Deuteronomy 6:4-9 suggests, one may find it beneficial to investigate generational and sociological studies. While no study seeks to pigeonhole all those born in a certain sequence of decades to rigid characteristics, a study can help to provide a general portrait of the preceding generation. Thom Rainer, and his son Jess, have sought to provide a helpful guide to understanding the Millennial generation through research and evaluation.

Thom Rainer is the president and CEO of LifeWay Christian Resources. He is the author of over twenty books, including *Simple Church* and *Surprising Insights from the Unchurched and Proven Ways to Reach Them*. Jess Rainer is an assistant pastor and banking professional. As is evident, the authors make up a father-son team, Thom being a member of the Baby Boomer generation, Jess being an older Millennial. Certainly, the family connection, as well as the divide generationally, offers a helpful and refreshing perspective to this type of study.

The volume is separated into eleven different chapters with an added postscript. Chapter one introduces the reader to what is now known as the Millennial generation. Jess Rainer authors the second chapter, offering a helpful perspective from within the generation itself. Chapters three through ten seek to draw correlations from the generational study, mapping what characteristics Millennials have in common with one another. Chapter eleven then seeks to offer a way forward in ministering to this generation, specifically from an ecclesiastical perspective.

One of the difficulties of this book may be found in its intended audience. While the entire book is premised on a study facilitated by the authors (4), there seems to be a reservation in detailing the research. For example, the authors state in regard to the study, "We could belabor all these points and bore you to death…" (5) and "We risk boring you with theses numbers…" (82) or another, "Forgive us if this excursion caused you to yawn" (9). There seems to be an assumption from the perspective of the author(s) that the reader will not be interested in the finer details of the study the book is built upon.

Further, the selection of the survey sample is worthy of attention. First, the book is seeking to articulate common characteristics among the Millennial generation. However, the study only covers those born between 1980 and 1991. In their own words, "our study is on the older Millennials" (4). To be sure, when the book was published in 2011, the youngest millennial, per their demarcations, would have been eleven and in the fourth grade. Nevertheless, a study seeking to articulate common components of a generation while only surveying half of that generation, could present difficulties. Second, one should note the generational delineation. According to the Rainers, Millennials are any of those born between 1980 and 2000. While this is within the general consensus of generational studies, some have argued for an exact year of 1982, and have allotted as late as 2004 as a final year.

Additionally, there were some elements that may have benefited from a more nuanced explanation. Jess Rainer, speaking about familial emphasis states, "Family values may well become one of the main distinguishing marks of the Millennials" (33). What is difficult in respect to "family values" is the lack of definition of this term within the book. One can speculate that the Millennial emphasis on monogamous, life-long marriages (63) is an affirmation of these values. Yet, the Millennial generation largely has no difficulty with same-sex marriage. This is only further confused when the author(s) states "[Millennials] desire to see their families return to *more traditional values*" (70, emphasis added). Therefore, the terms "family" and "traditional values" become cofounded, especially in contrast to popular nomenclature.

Jess Rainer also states that (primarily ethnic) diversity is "a nonissue" (35). While diversity and race relations have improved in the past half-century, to call this area a nonissue may be a misnomer. Chapter four is dedicated to evaluating the new openness among Millennials, particularly in regard to diversity. This is often contrasted with the actions and beliefs of former generations. Thus, while great strides have been made in areas of diversity, one may argue that Millennials are not blind to this issue. Certainly, even among Millennials—especially evangelicals—racial reconciliation and matters concerning diversity are important and vital topics.

With these elements in mind, pastors and organizational leaders may find *The Millennials* to be a useful volume in engaging with this multifaceted group of individuals. While virtually no one of this generation is a quintessential Millennial, having a broad understanding of their context and influences can help one better understand their, for lack of a better term, social consciousness. While the book is brief on any prescription, knowing the lay of the land allows each individual leader to formulate his or her path forward in this new generational discipleship.

For those involved in youth and family ministry, readers should be encouraged by the Rainer's findings. Particularly in chapter 3, "It's a Family Affair," the findings of the generational study are positive. While not perfect, Millennials seem to have a renewed emphasis on the importance of family. An overwhelming majority see themselves only being married once and staunchly against divorce. Further, a consistent theme found among this study was the Millennials' respect for older generations, especially their parents. According to the authors, "There is nothing more important to the Millennials than family" (76). For this, we should be thankful.

Youth Ministry in the 21st Century: Five Views. Edited by Chap Clark. Grand Rapids, MI: Baker Academic. 2015. 224 pp. $21.99. Paper.

Review by Charles Cook, Lead Pastor at Cookeville Free Will Baptist Church, Cookeville, Tennessee. He also serves as the editor for Randall House Academic Books, managing editor of *D6 Family Ministry Journal*, and teaches online courses for Randall University.

New collegiate ministries, national political engagement, and countless new hymns and choruses are among the many markers that define the post-World War Two American Evangelical movement. These ministries and movements serve as helpful tools for analyzing the impact and challenges faced by Christians, churches, and denominations that minister in today's context. Amidst all the sign posts of energized church life, ministry to youth continues to serve as one of the most important. With the strategic importance of youth work, it is unsurprising that numerous contemporary voices (parents, lay leaders, pastors, and parachurch) are engaged in revaluating the goals and foundations for youth specific ministry.

Into this realm of renewed evaluation, comes the recent book (2015) *Youth Ministry in the 21st Century*. With societal and personal forces demanding that those in youth ministry go deep and locate solid theological roots for the how and why of youth ministry, editor Chap Clark sets out to assist the Church in moving beyond youth groups that revolve around a few volunteers and a star youth pastor (xiii.) To provide this assistance, *Youth Ministry in the 21st Century* functions as a dialogue between five authors invested in youth ministry, who also possess thoughtful perspectives for revitalizing student ministry. The five authors are Chap Clark, Greg Stier, Brian Cosby, Fernando Arzola, and Ron Hunter. Their dialogue plays out in five sections, with each author laying out his youth ministry perspective followed by responses from the other four writers. The sections conclude with the original author briefly responding to the suggestions and critiques from the interlocutors.

Section one starts with Greg Stier, who is the founder and president of Dare 2 Share Ministries. Stier's approach "The Gospel Advancing View of Youth Ministry," seeks to move student ministry from program based models to lifestyle models, while keeping Evangelism and Discipleship connected (4). Stier's position accentuates the need to equip students to share the faith, the important role of stories, repetitive gospel sharing during youth gatherings, investing in the most willing teens, connecting all activities to the gospel, and reliance on prayer. Adults are encouraged to share in this type of ministry through modeling, coaching, and leadership embracement.

One of *Youth Ministry in the 21st Century's* strengths is in the carefully crafted responses to proposals. This is seen in section one when Brian Crosby raises concern that Stier relies too much on narrative passages of Scripture to undergird his approach, and (unintentionally?) undermines the role of God, local churches, and parents in youth ministry. Chap Clark issues similar concerns by reminding Stier and readers that God is the one who ultimately changes the world, and leaders should show students how to follow and experience His love (25). Fernando Arzola cautions that Stier's Gospel advancing strategy seems more like a formulaic imposition instead of a call to a deeper way of life. And finally, Ron Hunter echoes the other writers by encouraging Stier to develop deeper descriptions of discipleship than just simply sharing the faith.

Following Greg Stier, Brian Crosby a former youth pastor and the current pastor of Wayside Presbyterian Church, kicks off section two. Crosby utilizes his space to outline "The Reformed View of Youth Ministry." Arguing that youth ministry too often functions from an entertainment-driven foundation, Crosby pushes for student ministry to move instead toward a faithfulness based footing (41). To facilitate faithful student ministry, Crosby advocates a traditionally Reformed, means-of-grace approach. Therefore "The Reformed View of Youth Ministry" gives primacy to Word based ministry, prayer, sacraments, service, and community (43-49).

In the response to Crosby, this reviewer resonated most with the questions of Chap Clark and Ron Hunter. Clark identifies three important concerns for Crosby's ministry approach: the lack of appreciation for developmental differences between adults and adolescents, the amount of research indicating students do not default trust adults, and the low recognition in Crosby's position for how difficult it is for churches or individuals to go about enacting his suggested method. Ron Hunter, on the other hand, questions if Crosby's philosophy, that places almost all responsibility with church leadership, will not end up recreating the "hired-gun" and "superhero" youth pastor syndrome Crosby views negatively. In addition, Hunter correctly points out that Crosby's playing of faithfulness off against success is counterproductive and unclear. Success is not the antithesis of faithfulness, although some contrast the two in such a manner (65).

After section two's constructive back and forth, section three moves to Chap Clark's view titled "The Adoption View of Youth Ministry." Clark's view starts from the premise that many youth cease to exercise vibrant faith because churches fail to provide the most vita of resources, the community of faith (75). According to Clark, the mantra of long time youth worker Mike Yaconelli, "Jesus and kids; that's who we are, that's what we do," has served for decades as youth ministry's philosophical core, regardless of one's theological, denominational, or church background (77-78). From Clark's perspective, youth ministry's core foundation needs a renewed emphasis on the *corporate* identity of Jesus followers. This corporate identity, per Clark, finds biblical grounding in the New Testament's communal language. Words such as, assembly and body, and family terms such as, brother and sister, provide the narrative language for how Christians should see themselves and relate to one another. For teens to experience the communal support embodied in the New Testament, churches and youth groups must actively see that teens are adopted into the larger body. This is accomplished through strategic opportunities for worship and service. In Clark's adoption model, youth workers become bridges and guides for the fuller participation of teens in the church's corporate identity and mission.

Brian Crosby responds to Chap Clark's "Adoption View" with the pressing question, "Where's God's salvation, development, and sanctification of youth?" (97). To drive home his Godward concern, Crosby points out that Clark spends lots of space emphasizing loving one another, but the first command is to love God. Ron Hunter takes his response in a different direction, reminding readers that when students relocate for college, which many of them will do, their local church community does not move with them. It is imperative, therefore, that someone in the student's life guide them as they seek a new community of faith. Fernando Arzola does not spend much time critiquing Clark's view, but he does expand on Clark's emphasis on community. Which is fitting, because Arzola's section, which comes next, also has a thematic center fixed on community.

Arzola terms his communally focused fourth section "The Ecclesial View of Youth Ministry." This section begins with the wrenching observation that "Protestant youth ministry has all but deleted ecclesiology from its theological radar" (113). Arzola's view, which seeks to remedy the Protestant youth ministry's core deficiency differs strikingly from the other four perspectives. Instead of providing a distinct approach to youth ministry, Arzola challenges youth ministry to appropriate ancient church practices and to understand local ministry in light of the church universal's long history. To achieve this end, churches must *intentionally* perform their work under the rubric of the church as "one, holy, catholic, and apostolic," while simultaneously viewing local communities as Jesus' incarnated presence in the world where a renewed emphasis on universal church teaching and liturgy occurs (121-123).

Of all responses in *Youth Ministry in the 21st Century*, Greg Stier's rejoinder to "The Ecclesial View of Youth Ministry" stings the strongest. Holding back no punches, Stier responds that if "the subject of ancient creeds and pre-Reformation ecclesiology" comes to dominate youth gatherings, the four participants who happen to be present should have a great time (125). In no uncertain terms, Stier reminds readers that it is outward advance and sharing of the gospel that made the early church exciting, not "developing, dissecting, and distributing creeds" (125). The starkness of Stier's response is refreshing, even if it is also somewhat overblown. Nonetheless, strong responses serve in this book as a reminder that the subject matter…matters! The other responders to Arzola are not as critical, Ron Hunter's response highlights the lack of uniformity among early church fathers as a helpful antidote to Arzola's wishful thinking on early church doctrinal unity, and several authors question the lack of practicality in putting Arzola's view into practice.

The fifth and final view, "The D6 View of Youth Ministry" grounds its presentation not in Arzola's ancient church practices, but in the scriptural commands of Deuteronomy 6. Ron Hunter, the CEO of Randall House publications and co-founder of the D6 conference, offers up a vision of

Youth ministry where parents and church workers work together intentionally to minister to students. To enact the D6 approach, Hunter lays out five focal points: Be a Transformational Leader / Build a Strategic Philosophy / Build a Team Approach Among Staff With Volunteers / Teach Students / Coach Parents to Be Coaches. One of Hunter's strengths, like several other contributors, was repeated reliance on Scripture to guide his proposal.

Despite a solid scriptural foundation, a common response to "The D6 Model" stresses its inadequacy in dealing with 21st century family breakdown. How, several responders wondered, will Hunter's emphasis on church and family partnerships deal effectively with the multidimensional reality of modern family life. In addition to those concerns, Crosby raised again in his response his consistent concern that "The D6 Model" also overly roots itself in what humans can do and not in what God does. Furthermore, Crosby's response wonders why youth ministers are viewed as heroes in the D6 view, but no mention of God as ultimate hero.

For those seeking to understand the contemporary state of Student Ministry, *Youth Ministry in the 21st Century* has made a timely arrival. Likewise, for those looking to strengthen or retool ministry to students, this book provides a starting point for grasping some of the most thoughtful perspectives currently available. Readers will discover in its pages the scriptural foundations and philosophic insights that undergird youth ministries current re-envisioning. As with most multi-authored works, some sections are stronger than others, but the insightful back and forth with responders makes each section worthwhile. All these reasons and more make *Youth Ministry in the 21st Century* a book well worth investing in and learning from.

A family-aligned curriculum for every generation!

aligns all ages of the family

D6 CURRICULUM aligns small group environments at church so the entire family from kindergarten to grandparents, is studying the same theme at the same time. D62GEN helps parents and grandparents connect with kids and teens (even if they are miles away) through the use of devotional study guides, Splink, Home Connection, and other take-home resources that help equip the home.

D62Gen connects the church and home through generational discipleship.

www.d62gen.com

BASED ON DEUTERONOMY 6:5-9

Family Ministry Resources

from  randall house

The Beautiful Chaos of Parenting Teens

by Leneita Fix

Wit and wisdom to help you parent through the teen years

ISBN: 9780892659906
PRICE: $14.99

Five Reasons for Spiritual Apathy in Teens

by Rob & Amy Rienow

What can parents do to help spiritual apathy in teens?

ISBN: 9780892659883
PRICE: $9.99

Practical Family Ministry

by Timothy Paul Jones and John David Trentham

A collection of practical family ministry ideas for you to implement in your church

ISBN: 9780892659876
PRICE: $13.99

The DNA of D6

by Ron Hunter

The DNA of D6 shares great strategies for all family ministries. It builds on the foundation of a timeless philosophy found in Deuteronomy 6.

ISBN: 9780892656554
PRICE: $14.99

Relentless Parenting

by Brian and Angela Haynes

Find hope and encouragement to keep parenting teens, even when the road gets tough

ISBN: 9780892659890
PRICE: $14.99

Surviving Culture Parent Edition

by Edward E. Moody

When Character and Your World Collide

ISBN: 9780892659838
PRICE: $9.99

• • More titles available at D6FAMILY.COM • •

www.ingramcontent.com/pod-product-compliance
Lightning Source LLC
Chambersburg PA
CBHW070809230426
43665CB00017B/2541